Performance Measurement Explained

Designing and Implementing
Your State-of-the-Art System

Also available from ASQ Quality Press:

Root Cause Analysis: Simplified Tools and Techniques
Bjørn Andersen and Tom Fagerhaug

Business Process Improvement Toolbox
Bjørn Andersen

Staffing the New Workplace: Selecting and Promoting for Quality Improvement
Ronald B. Morgan and Jack E. Smith

High Quality Leadership: Practical Guidelines to Becoming a More Effective Manager
Erwin Rausch and John B. Washbush

Let's Work Smarter, Not Harder: How to Engage Your Entire Organization in the Execution of Change
Michael Caravatta

The Change Agents' Handbook: A Survival Guide for Quality Improvement Champions
David W. Hutton

Value Leadership: Winning Competitive Advantage in the Information Age
Michael C. Harris

Creativity, Innovation, and Quality
Paul E. Plsek

To request a complimentary catalog of ASQ Quality Press publications, call 800-248-1946, or visit our Web site at http://qualitypress.asq.org .

Performance Measurement Explained

Designing and Implementing
Your State-of-the-Art System

Bjørn Andersen
Tom Fagerhaug

ASQ Quality Press
Milwaukee, Wisconsin

Performance Measurement Explained: Designing and Implementing Your State-of-the-Art System
Bjørn Andersen and Tom Fagerhaug

Library of Congress Cataloging-in-Publication Data

Andersen, Bjørn.
  Performance measurement explained : designing and implementing your state-of-the-art system / Bjørn Andersen, Tom Fagerhaug.
      p. cm.
  Includes bibliographical references and index.
  ISBN 0-87389-520-7 (pbk. : alk. paper)
  1. Personnel management. 2. Performance—Management. I. Fagerhaug, Tom, 1968– II. Title.

  HF5549 .A816 2001
  658.3'125—dc21   2001004984

10 9 8 7 6 5 4 3 2 1

ISBN 0-87389-520-7

Acquisitions Editor: Annemieke Koudstaal
Project Editor: Craig S. Powell
Production Administrator: Gretchen Trautman
Special Marketing Representative: David Luth

ASQ Mission: The American Society for Quality advances individual, organizational, and community excellence worldwide through learning, quality improvement, and knowledge exchange.

Attention Bookstores, Wholesalers, Schools, and Corporations: ASQ Quality Press books, videotapes, audiotapes, and software are available at quantity discounts with bulk purchases for business, educational, or instructional use. For information, please contact ASQ Quality Press at 800-248-1946, or write to ASQ Quality Press, P.O. Box 3005, Milwaukee, WI 53201-3005.

To place orders or to request a free copy of the ASQ Quality Press Publications Catalog, including ASQ membership information, call 800-248-1946. Visit our Web site at www.asq.org or http://qualitypress.asq.org .

Printed in the United States of America

∞ Printed on acid-free paper

American Society for Quality

ASQ

Quality Press
600 N. Plankinton Avenue
Milwaukee, Wisconsin 53203
Call toll free 800-248-1946
Fax 414-272-1734
www.asq.org
http://qualitypress.asq.org
http://standardsgroup.asq.org
E-mail: authors@asq.org

Table of Contents

Preface

What is performance, and why would you want to measure it? If you look up the word *performance* in a dictionary, several different meanings are presented. In the context of this book, the correct meaning is explained by the use of words such as *efficiency, accomplishment,* and so on. In the world of business, this translates into a measure of how well various activities are carried out to produce a certain level of performance. As we will explain later, there are many different reasons why you would want to measure your level of performance, but let's briefly look at some other definitions provided by a dictionary.

The word *performance* is believed to have originated in the fifteenth century to mean a play or exhibition of some type. Today, this meaning of the word covers not only cultural events like concerts and theater plays, but also includes sporting events, which is the direction in which we want to turn your attention for a minute. What is the key feature of sports? Besides the idealistic objectives of staying fit, a sound mind in a sound body, and so on, the core of any sport is competition through measurement of performance.

Whether the athletes run, jump, sail, score goals, or whatever type of activity is performed, some means for measuring the better athlete or team exist, be they measuring time, distance, goals, points, and so on. Why have people throughout the centuries been spending time and energy on activities like sports, which, per se, are a waste? Obviously because it gives them something in terms of personal motivation and pleasure. This stems not only from the many positive effects of sports, for example, the aforementioned sound body and social relations with other people, but also from the fact that sports, based on measurement of performance, give instant and clear feedback on how well you are at various activities.

When people go to work, they rarely receive such a direct type of feedback on their performance. Granted, in certain lines of work, you might—salespeople can count the amount of dollars they have personally generated, service staff have first-hand contact with customers and receive feedback from them, and so on. But on the average, employees rarely get the opportunity to "compete" and measure their performance in the execution of their jobs. All experiences with performance measurement systems do, however, tell the same story: exposure to continuous and operational performance measurement can introduce some of the same thrills provided by sports.

This is certainly no black-and-white picture indicating that some type of measurement at work is good and no measurement is bad. We have definitely seen examples of performance measurement that achieved nothing good—where the measurements were used to control and manipulate employees. This does not reflect the core intentions and purposes of measurement. When the performance measurements are geared toward providing the kind of feedback that people seek when engaging in sports, they have the potential to excite people and make them look forward to the next "competition" with anticipation. They might even start to "train" for the next event, that is, try to figure out and implement ways to improve their performance, much like athletes adjust their technique, equipment, and mental approaches. When this competition mode settles in, there are really no limits as to how far people can push their levels of performance.

Among all the effects that can be reaped from a sound performance measurement system, this is probably the most compelling and striking manifestation. If this book can inspire you to design and implement your own state-of-the-art performance measurement system, we have truly achieved our goals in writing this book.

From the very outset, this was intended to be a practical book, aimed at providing a "recipe" on how to develop and implement a modern performance measurement system. We hope we have succeeded at this, even though we feel the need to start the book with three chapters of a more introductory nature. These initial chapters will take you through some background on performance measurement, the applications it has in industry, and our proposal for an alternative management model based on performance measurement data.

The first three chapters also set the stage for the main part of the book, a run-through of an eight-step process for designing and implementing a performance measurement system. We have divided the treatment of this process into one chapter per step, and our objective through these chapters has been to give you clear and practical advice and insight into how you can determine your own performance measurement system. It is our sincere hope that this "recipe" will prove sufficient for you to accomplish this task. In this section of the book, we have included a small graphic navigational aid in the upper corners of the pages. This section also includes an extensive example of an organization we recently worked with as they designed and implemented their performance measurement system. At the end of each chapter of this eight-step process, there is a summary of how this company completed the step in question.

Following the run-through of this design and implementation process, a final chapter attempts to show you a few examples of how you can apply your new performance measurement system for different purposes. At the end of the book, you will also find a brief literature list for further reading. However, as you will be able to tell when reading the book, we have not emphasized the academic style of writing with references scattered densely about. If you seek more information on a particular topic and are unable to locate it, please contact us and we will see if we can point you in the right direction. Finally, at the very end, we have included a list of some possible performance indicators within various areas and for different business processes. These are mainly meant to be inspiration for your own efforts at tailoring indicators to your own specific needs.

We would like to include our most sincere acknowledgments to the organizations we have been fortunate enough to work with during their struggles to put performance measurement to use. Without the lessons learned from them, we would never have been able to write this book. Finally, we are forever grateful to our spouses for bearing with us and the clatter of our keyboards on late evenings, and to Hilde for proofreading!

We truly hope you will enjoy this book, and we welcome any comments or suggestions for improvement!

Trondheim, Norway, July, 2001

Bjørn Andersen   Tom Fagerhaug
Bjorn.Andersen@ipk.ntnu.no   Tom.Fagerhaug@indman.sintef.no

Chapter 1

A Brief History of Performance Measurement

The principles that apply in designing a state-of-the-art performance measurement system of today rely on experience gained through trial and error throughout the last century. Thus, it is pertinent to quickly recap the most important lessons learned in this respect.

1.1 DEVELOPMENT OF THE PRODUCTIVITY CONCEPT

The history of performance and performance measurement really starts with the history of productivity and productivity measurement, which became relevant concepts starting with the industrial revolution. From village communities where products and services were custom-made for every client in a very labor-intensive fashion, mass production gradually became possible. This extremely important transition, which truly constitutes the basis for our present high living standard, at least materially speaking, is also to blame for the less fortunate developments of productivity, and performance, measurement. Let's take a look at the major phases of industrial production:

The English System of Manufacture

• First, the English System of Manufacture, stretching from 1800 to 1850, where the ethos was accuracy. Parts were made one at a time, for one product, to fit exactly together. Perfection was the objective, and the better the fit, the better the workmanship. Even though productivity increased dramatically compared to earlier methods, manufacturing was still quite inefficient and labor intensive.

The American System of Manufacture

- Around 1850, the American System of Manufacture evolved, based on both perfection and interchangeability of parts. This led to the separation of operations from one another, so that parts could be produced in larger quantities and, thus, more efficiently. Again, productivity leaped from the level of the former stage, but was still relatively low.

The Taylor System

- Toward the end of the nineteenth century, Frederick W. Taylor realized that worker-related activities were limiting the speed and efficiency that could be achieved by the more-than-capable machines of the time. This realization led to the Taylor System and the scientific management stage, which focused on controlling human activities in order to increase labor productivity.

Transition from craftsmanship to industrial productivity

- At this point, the transition from craftsmanship to industrial productivity was completed. Expensive machines that had to be kept running were being installed. To justify the high capital investments, machine utilization needed to be high. As human activities limited the utilization rate, labor efficiency had to increase accordingly. Industrial productivity became synonymous with machine utilization and labor efficiency, the latter being achieved through tools such as the conveyor belt, time and motion studies, reliance on the learning curve, and so on.

- During the nineteenth century, people were able to buy finished goods fresh out of modern factories for the first time in history. The slope of technological development was steeper than it had ever been before, leading to cascades of entirely new products being launched more and more frequently. People bought these products, and management was challenged to increase worker productivity and replace obsolete work methods and equipment with newer, more expensive equipment, while simultaneously developing and introducing new products. All in all, the key focus was efficiency—of workers and machines.

Two world wars

- The next century encountered two world wars. For decades after they ended, these wars created truly extraordinary conditions for industry. The world markets were nearly insatiable and consumed products of almost any quality. Again, the challenges were to drive the technological development ahead, mainly on the premises of the developers. Very rarely were the customers asked what they wanted. Still, companies survived this negligence of customer needs mainly because consumers were more oriented toward quantity than quality. Based on the belief that success with innovative products could offset poor performance in traditional operations, productivity was still synonymous with efficiency, that is, labor productivity and machine utilization.

Productivity = labor efficiency + machine utilization

If you think we have repeatedly mentioned that productivity throughout the decades has focused on labor productivity and machine utilization, let us assure you it has been for a purpose—this became the prevailing productivity paradigm for a very long time, dictating the principles for measuring productivity accordingly. We will shortly see some examples of emphasis placed on high-level efficiency measures, very often of a financial nature. The prevalence of this efficiency paradigm has become more viable due to the immense support it has received from accounting systems. The principles for financial and accounting systems were developed during the extraordinary circumstances of the industrial revolution, very rapid technological development, and the two world wars we just discussed. These principles are still very much alive today and impact how organizations measure.

1.2 FROM PRODUCTIVITY TO PERFORMANCE

Productivity is measured as a ratio

Alongside the gradual establishment of the efficiency paradigm of productivity, the concept of *productivity measurement* was developed. Productivity has been measured for decades, if not centuries, in increasingly sophisticated ways. It started with the very simple relationship between input and output of the process, system, or organization being measured, and is usually expressed as a ratio. The most general definition was, much like a utilization ratio for different types of energy consumption:

$$\text{Productivity} = \frac{\text{Output}}{\text{Input}}$$

Formula for total productivity

Output and input would almost exclusively be measured in monetary values, and the ratio would produce a number between 0 and 1, thus being very easy to understand. Further, it could quite easily be adapted to the desired level of aggregation—for the organization as a whole, subprocesses, departments, and so on—as well as to the different factors of output and input that were being measured. One typical measure would be:

$$\text{Total productivity} = \frac{\text{Added value}}{\left(\begin{array}{c}\text{Direct labor}\\\text{costs} +\\\text{Social costs}\end{array}\right) + \left(\begin{array}{c}\text{Indirect labor}\\\text{costs} +\\\text{Social costs}\end{array}\right) + \text{Cost of capital}}$$

By the way, when discussing levels of aggregation, please observe that we limit our treatment of productivity measurement to organizations and avoid any discussion regarding productivity measurement at the country or regional levels, which is an entirely different matter dominated more by economists.

When this conveniently simple definition of productivity was developed, the ideal of the time was to arrive at a measurement system where you could measure productivity, according to the output over input definition, at a few key spots in the organization. Through simple, purely mathematical calculations these measures could in turn be aggregated into one, single overall productivity figure for the entire organization. This became a strikingly simple entity to handle, interpret, compare, and, consequently, pursue. How much value do you think this added to the management of such organizations? At the time, when efficiency of labor and machines were the most important aspects of the operation, they probably did work fairly well. The point we want to make by taking you through this history lesson is that it does not work today, when competitive conditions have changed immensely.

Figure 1.1 attempts to illustrate that an aggregated productivity measure, which in close to 100 percent of cases is based on accounting data, is as useful for running an organization as trying to drive a car by looking in the rearview mirror and turning the wheel based on the image of the road you see there. It presents information about events that occurred in the past, very often way back in the past, and it provides no more details than a traffic light regarding whether or not you are doing OK or if you are at risk of going from OK to not OK.

Formulas for partial productivity measures   Since our predecessors in this area were certainly not blind to this, so-called partial productivity measures were developed when they realized that these highly aggregated, simple measures did not provide enough details to be useful. Although retaining the tradition of output over input

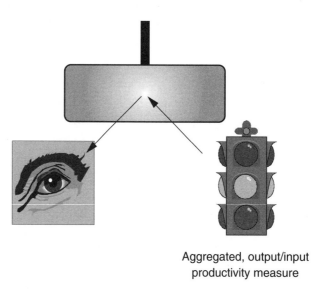

Aggregated, output/input
productivity measure

Figure 1.1 Aggregated productivity measures are lagging measures.

definitions and basing them on accounting data, the partial productivity measures enabled measuring the productivity of subareas—more specific activities than the entire organization at once.

Some partial productivity measures were:

- Labor productivity = $\dfrac{\text{Added value}}{\text{Direct labor costs} + \text{Social costs}}$

- Productivity of capital = $\dfrac{\text{Added value}}{\text{Cost of capital}}$

- Productivity of energy = $\dfrac{\text{Added value}}{\text{Cost of energy}}$

- Productivity of input goods = $\dfrac{\text{Added value}}{\text{Cost of input goods}}$

As the post–World War II rebuilding approached completion and the demand caused by years of non-normal production was met, ordinary competitive conditions were introduced for the first time in a long, long time. Any new products that were introduced no longer dazzled customers, and the market changed from being the seller's to becoming the buyer's. Customers could compare a large number of offers and choose among them. Buying criteria other than price came into consideration, criteria that the traditional productivity paradigm was no longer able to satisfy.

Around the middle of the 1980s, this led to the introduction of the term "performance" as a replacement for "productivity," which seemed to have outlived its role. In 1989, Sink and Tuttle published one of the first approaches to performance measurement in their book *Planning and Measurement in Your Organization of the Future* . Their theory went far beyond the simple output/input relationships employed previously and claimed that the performance of an organizational system is a complex interrelationship between seven different criteria, as shown in Figure 1.2.

Introduction of the term performance

This performance model represented a realization that for an organization to perform well and stay competitive, it had to excel in a number of areas, including, but not limited to, being productive. Throughout the 1980s and 1990s, several different performance models were introduced to explain even better what factors make up the performance of an organization. Some of the best known are: the more comprehensive balanced scorecard approach developed by Kaplan and Norton (1996), which we will discuss in more detail later on in the book; simpler models by Lynch and Cross (1991) and others; and in Europe, some approaches developed in cross-European research projects, for instance AMBITE and ENAPS (for a description of these, consult the Web site of the European Commission's research programs: www.cordis.lu).

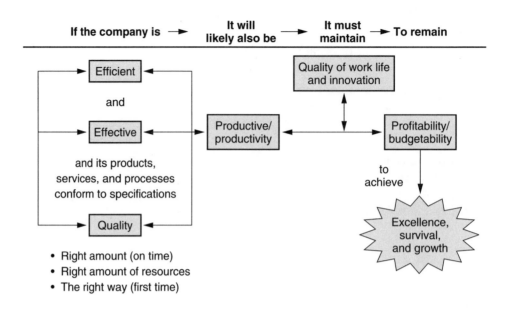

Figure 1.2   The performance equation presented by Sink and Tuttle.

Source: D. S. Sink and T. C. Tuttle, *Planning and Measurement in Your Organization of the Future* (Norcross, VA: Industrial Engineering and Management Press, 1989). Reprinted with the permission of the Institute of Industrial Engineers, 25 Technology Park, Norcross, GA 30092, 770-449-0461.

There is no generally accepted definition of performance

Currently, there is no one, generally accepted definition of what constitutes performance. In fact, it is probably not useful to strive for one either, as this varies over time, from industry to industry and, probably, from region to region. We believe it is sufficient to have reached a point where performance has replaced productivity and is generally accepted to cover a wide range of aspects of an organization—from the old productivity to the ability to innovate, to attract the best employees, to maintain an environmentally sound outfit, or to conduct business in an ethical manner. How to measure these concepts will be discussed later. For now, let us move on to a discussion about why you should measure, whether all measurement is good, and how measurement might affect those being measured.

Chapter 2

The Purpose, Psychology, and Perils of Performance Measurement

Before we start this chapter, let us try to eliminate any confusion that might arise throughout this book due to imprecise use of the following two concepts: *performance measures* and *performance indicators*. Normally, we use the term *performance measure* when talking about performance measurement in general, as in some kind of measurement being made. We refer to *performance indicator* as a more specific measurement, that is, a gauge or, well, an indicator. As this brief account clearly demonstrates, the distinction between these two is not completely clear—try to bear with us!

Performance measures versus performance indicators

2.1 WHY MEASURE PERFORMANCE?

As we tried to demonstrate in the preface of this book, one important purpose of performance measurement is to provide employees with feedback on the work they are performing, just as different sports activities provide feedback on athletic skill. Feedback from employees can generate many potentially positive effects, such as improving motivation or launching improvement initiatives. There are, however, several different reasons why you should measure performance in your organization, and we will quickly take you through some of them (if for no other reason than to convince you that it is worthwhile to implement a performance measurement system in your organization and give you ammunition in your struggle to convince others).

Performance measurement provides a general information basis that can be exploited for decision-making purposes, both for management and for all levels of employees. In this capacity, the performance measurement system can become the instrument panel, or cockpit, that is necessary to

Performance measurement as an instrument panel

replace the rearview mirror approach offered by the traditional accounting system–based measurements. This instrument panel is used for strategic maneuvering, day-to-day running of the organization, and planning and implementing improvements and changes. As opposed to the rearview mirror approach illustrated in Figure 1.1, the performance measurement system becomes more like the kind of situation required for steering your car, boat, or plane, with a course charted (the organization's strategy), an instrument panel with gages providing you with the necessary information about the vehicle and its movements, and a steering wheel (which in the organization's case can be decisions, improvement projects, behavior-altering performance measurements, and so on). This is roughly depicted in Figure 2.1.

Since the performance measurement system keeps your eyes on the road instead of looking through the rearview mirror, its function as an early warning system should not be underestimated. Figure 2.2 illustrates this function. One simplified cause-and-effect chain starts with the development of knowledge inside the organization. This knowledge, in turn, is employed to develop and perform business processes, which then create products or services that achieve some level of performance in the marketplace. This leads to a final financial result, either good or bad. Typically, there is a considerable time lag from the initial knowledge development, through each of these links, until the financial result appears. The organization will have had plenty of time to establish many bad decisions and actions before you

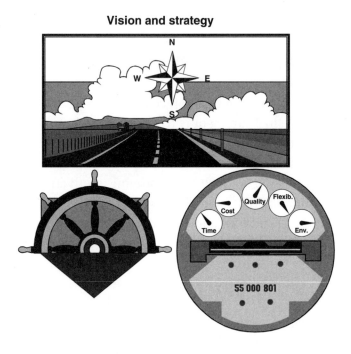

Figure 2.1 The view of the organization's "drive" when a performance measurement system is used as an instrument panel.

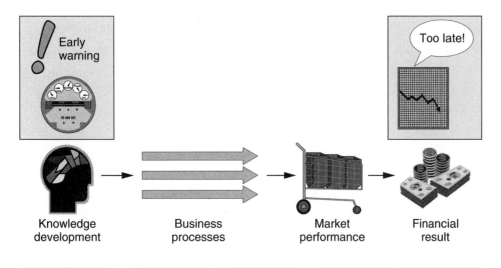

Figure 2.2   Performance measurement as an early warning system.

can read it on the financial statement. Therefore, the accounting system is not a good tool for monitoring performance for the purpose of taking action when things take a turn for the worse. Focusing on market performance gives you an early warning, even earlier if you measure your business process performance. Perhaps the earliest warning comes from monitoring your basic knowledge development inside the organization, and is often a year or two ahead of when the accounting red light goes off. An operational performance measurement system is a very effective early warning system that you really cannot do without.

Performance measurement as an early warning

As previously mentioned, performance measurement has a great ability to alter the behavior of individuals, groups, or whole organizations, and can thus be used to promote desired changes. This is a psychological fact that can be exploited when designing performance measurement systems to stimulate actions that will benefit the organization, as in this striking example: A large newspaper company printed the newspaper during the night, and made use of the presses during the day to print jobs for various external customers. These jobs were scheduled for printing and delivery on agreed-upon dates, although nothing was said about what specific time of day. For a long time, the company struggled to complete the jobs on the predetermined day. Overtime was usually required to finish the jobs, and customers charged penalties for tardy deliveries. Even after improvements were made to increase the equipment's reliability, the jobs consistently ran into overtime, leading management to hypothesize that perhaps the press operators had grown so accustomed to the overtime pay that they were, deliberately or unconsciously, pushing the jobs into overtime. To test the theory, management began to measure what portion of jobs was completed within regular

Performance measurement can alter behavior

working hours. In parallel, a new system of dividing a bonus among the operators was introduced, based on how much money in tardiness penalties was saved compared with the average penalties incurred before this system was launched. Within a few weeks, almost every single job was finished on time.

Performance measurement for implementing strategies and policies

Due to this behavior-altering ability, defining performance measures is one way of implementing strategies and policies. For each element of a strategic plan, key performance indicators can be defined. These can then be broken down into performance measures at the business process or department levels. Since these measures will normally stimulate behavior in a direction encouraged by the organization, this will contribute to an alignment toward the same goals and objectives.

Performance measurement for trend monitoring

The performance data captured by the performance measurement system can be used to monitor development over time, that is, the performance trend. In general, enterprises amass enormous amounts of data and information, and financial records are the best-documented part. Such data are often used to undertake analyses of different types of cause-and-effect relationships. Storing historical performance data can be an even more powerful source for analytical approaches. For instance, in hindsight, a correlation can be found between the performance levels of certain processes and the resulting customer satisfaction data, or a link can be discovered between profitability for certain accounting periods and characteristics of the operations at that time. This can then provide important insight into how things should be done in the future.

Performance measurement for improvement prioritization

Linked to such monitoring of performance trends, performance measurement can be utilized to identify business processes, areas, departments, and so on, that need to be improved to keep up with demands. We could write an entire book about improvement of business processes (in fact, we already have) and why it is absolutely necessary for staying in the game. Suffice it to say that every organization must constantly be alert to the need for improvement, and systematic performance measurement forms a solid foundation for deciding where improvements are most pertinent at any given time.

Performance measurement for improvement project evaluation

After improvement projects are completed, performance measurement can be used for assessing whether they actually produced the projected results, which in turn makes it easier to design later projects for a better success rate. Very often, improvement projects, along with any other type of project or investment, will be subjected to some type of investment justification requirements. Existing justification mechanisms, not surprisingly, were designed by accountants and economists and are based on return ratios, payback times, and so on. The problem with these approaches is that improvement projects often generate more intangible or operational gains, gains not necessarily easily converted into monetary figures (this is often referred to as, respectively, green and blue savings, and will be discussed later in this book). Being able to document the operational performance improvements produced through such projects can effectively deflect tough questions from the "bean counters."

It is becoming more and more common that companies require their suppliers to document performance levels for a number of different aspects of their operations. Even in tendering or bidding situations for parts or services contracts, which are either of high importance to the customer or are long-term, the prospective vendor is typically asked to document previous performance. Having a performance measurement system in place makes complying with such requirements easier and much more trustworthy than having to haphazardly rustle something together on short notice. Taking this further, data from a performance measurement system can be used actively in marketing. If you consistently achieve a very high level of product quality, short delivery times, or superior environmental performance, this can be one way you convince potential customers to choose your offer.

Performance measurement data as a marketing tool

Incentive, bonus, and pay systems can be linked to performance measurement, which awards benefits for true achievements. An office furniture manufacturer with about 300 employees took advantage of this aspect of performance measurement. Displaying consistent delivery rates in the upper 80th percentile, the company started an in-house campaign. All employees with a direct impact on the delivery rate were identified; for each delivery rate percentage point gained above 90 by the end of the year (and kept there for at least three weeks in a row), two all-expenses paid trips to the Super Bowl were drawn in a raffle. By Christmas, the delivery rate was up to 98 percent!

Performance measurement as input into bonus and incentive systems

Performance data can form the basis for benchmarking against other organizations, either competitors or others. As we will discuss in more detail later, one problem with strictly internal performance measurement is that the measurements are entirely relative. There is no fixed reference to indicate how good, comparatively, the performance is; therefore the measurement trend is the most useful aspect to keep an eye on. If measurements are compared with the performance levels of other organizations through benchmarking, a reference can be established that enables setting targets for different performance measures based on what others have achieved.

Performance measurement as a basis for benchmarking

As described in the preface, the implementation of a well-functioning performance measurement system, if used in the right way, can help motivate the organization through the feedback it can provide to individuals and departments. Thus, there are an abundance of reasons why you should measure performance in your organization. You should be aware, though, that performance measurement might also cause some unexpected effects, mainly due to the psychological impact that being measured can have on some people.

Performance measurement for increased motivation

2.2 PSYCHOLOGICAL EFFECTS OF PERFORMANCE MEASUREMENT

This section's heading was chosen to indicate that we are not so naïve that we believe performance measurement is a golden path to eternal success that encounters no problems or obstacles. While the purpose of the heading is pertinent, it is still not entirely accurate. Performance measurement, as such, has very few psychological (or any other) effects attached to it, it is merely a neutral process of collecting data. What brings about effects, either positive (as outlined in the previous section) or negative, is how these data are treated afterwards; that is, the processing or evaluation of the collected performance data. This activity can indeed have some negative psychological effects attached to it.

Punishment must be avoided for performance measurement at the individual level

The initial, most obvious effect occurs if an unfortunate combination of measurement level and data processing is put into place. This combination consists of measurement right down to a personal level and uses the measurements for punishment or other types of negative feedback. First, measurement at the personal level means either: collecting performance data about processes or activities impacted by only one individual, so that it is obvious who is the source for the measured—good or bad— performance level; or connecting performance data to one person who is not the only one, or is not at all, responsible for the performance level in question. Second, inappropriate use allows management, either an immediate superior or someone higher up in the hierarchy, to exploit the performance data as some kind of leverage toward an employee, either to make that person work harder, to withhold pay, or simply to mock him or her. Measurement at the individual level (if used right) need not be negative, but in the hands of manipulative or even "psychopathic" management, it has the potential to ruin the work situation for the persons being measured.

We have certainly seen examples of this extremely negative type of performance measurement, and we therefore take this opportunity to warn you against designing your performance measurement system in a manner that allows such situations to arise. While there might very well be cases where individual measurement is warranted, for example, where different business processes are mainly controlled by one person or where the pay and bonus system links individual performance to economic rewards, you should think twice whenever the establishment of such measurement is contemplated.

Other psychological effects, which are usually less prominent, occur less often, or have less pronounced consequences, are:

Over-stimulation of overachievers

• Too much stimulation of, or the creation of, overachievers. Some people are—or might become—quite prone to giving their very all to achieve the best possible result. Such people are normally an extremely useful asset for any organization, but there have been examples where the introduction of performance measurement has nurtured this instinct to the extent that it has become unhealthy. In such cases, there is an imminent risk of burn-out from becoming completely engrossed with work and pushing those measures ever higher. If you suspect something like this is happening, you should consider having a serious talk with the person in question, moving the person to a different position, or possibly abandoning the measurements, at least for a while.

• When people are not accustomed to having their performance levels directly measured, as enabled by a state-of-the-art performance measurement system, being measured can often feel threatening, at least in the beginning—before management has proven that the measurements will be utilized for positive purposes (see the first problem mentioned in this section). An extension of this issue is that some people become very good at finding excuses as to why performance levels are low or declining, thus not identifying the real reasons and doing something about them. Usually, this is a matter of trust and allows employees to see that the measurements can be used for something good. The funny thing about such situations is that the people who distrust the measurements when they are bad often place much faith in them when they are good!

Finding excuses for low performance levels

• As part of performance measurement implementation, some organizations define performance targets for their business processes, departments, activities, or even individual persons. In theory, this should be a welcome addition, since it not only provides feedback but also tells people what is expected of them. The problem is that targets very often are perceived as ceilings for performance. When the target level is reached, or even approached, people slow down and cease to strive for further improvement. On the other hand, since targets provide an objective to maneuver toward, they do offer some positive effects. So if you want to combine measurements with targets, make sure these targets are sufficiently ambitious to pose a real challenge (without being impossible to reach), and make it clear that the targets are meant to be constantly revised (motivation for reaching ever-higher targets can be provided by attaching some kind of bonus or other incentive to the attainment of the targets).

Targets can become ceilings for performance

• Finally, after implementing performance measurement, people quickly become used to the existence of continuous feedback. If the measurements either do not cover all areas or processes they work in, or are not functioning for a period of time, they often experience a void when there is no such feedback. This is not a major problem, but it can be avoided by systematically establishing performance measures for all or most of the important activities of the organization.

Performance measurement creates expectations for feedback in all situations

To conclude this section, we would like to present two "old truths" that definitely no longer apply:

• Precision is essential for useful measurement. This might be true for very technical types of measurement or even for accounting purposes, but not for operational performance measurement. The purpose of such performance measurement is to provide trend feedback, that is, whether developments are positive or negative, or whether improvement efforts produce results, not to measure performance with immaculate accuracy. Allocating too many resources to the development of painstakingly precise and accurate measurement systems can actually delay and obstruct the introduction of a practical system that works. A somewhat more pragmatic attitude is required in this respect.

• Subjective measures are sloppy. Many people strongly believe that measurement is performed by measuring: time by using a stopwatch, dimensions by using a measuring device of some sort, monetary value by counting money, and so on—some way of neutrally and objectively determining the value of the measure in question. However, very often the most useful measures are not of this type, for example, the quality of work life, the product's ability to satisfy customer needs, or the capability for innovation. These are more subjective measures that provide valuable insight, but must be measured through some indirect approach, for example by asking a person her or his opinion on a scale from 1 to 10, by using a surrogate indicator, or with some other means. Such subjective measures are not sloppy or less worthy than objective measures, they are simply of a different nature. Both hold a place in a state-of-the-art performance measurement system.

2.3 PERFORMANCE MEASURES CAN BE WRONG

A final word in terms of introductory warnings—performance measures can be wrong! Hastily defined performance measures, and sometimes even more carefully designed ones, can measure the wrong things and drive behavior in an unwanted direction, measure incorrectly, or produce varying precision over time. The first issue is a matter of understanding which behavior you want to promote and defining measures that support it, the latter two are questions of validity and reliability. Without going into the depths of an academic explanation, validity reports on the ability to correctly measure what is supposed to be measured, for example, whether the measure "number of active participants in a discussion session" is able to say something about the quality of the air in the meeting room where the session took place. Reliability addresses a measure's ability to produce the same value over time, for example how well a gage returns the same value throughout the day if what it is measuring remains unchanged.

All of these three issues, that is, the desired behavior you want to stimulate, validity, and reliability, must be addressed in the design of the performance measurement system, specifically when designing the detailed performance indicators to be used. To illustrate what the failure to address these potential problems can create, we have included some more or less striking examples following:

The first might be more of a legend than an actual occurrence, but it clearly shows how dire the consequences can become when performance measures are defined without considering their potential side effects. In a farming collective in the former Soviet Union, a manager won the contest for highest slaughter weight three years in a row . . . the fourth year he committed suicide, since he had killed all the breeding animals.

A more familiar example involves an electronics manufacturer. The performance indicator "development in procurement prices" was introduced to measure the performance of a procurement manager and his department. During the first year, he was able to save considerable amounts of money through spot buying and playing different bidders against each other. The only problem was that manufacturing costs increased by 10 times the saved amount of money due to late deliveries, defects, and other quality problems of purchased parts.

In terms of lacking validity, many well-meaning performance indicators are especially fooled by changes in volumes or mix of products or services delivered or activities performed. For instance, another manufacturer of electronic equipment reduced its production volume by 12.5 percent during a period of close follow-up of unit manufacturing costs. Since the largest portion of the manufacturing costs was fixed (independent of volume), the unit cost "increased" by 14 percent. Due to efforts to reduce the need for time-consuming testing because of better cooperation with selected suppliers, the true manufacturing time and cost per unit had decreased considerably. Similarly, a cable manufacturer experienced declining sales measured in the number of sold yards of cable. At the same time, sales revenues were maintained by steering the customers toward thicker and more advanced, and thus more expensive, types of cables. The performance measurement issued a warning that unit costs were increasing, while productivity and income were actually showing a positive trend.

Reliability is a performance indicator's ability to produce the correct value consistently over time

Hopefully, this chapter has demonstrated that there are many pitfalls to watch out for when designing a performance measurement system. The next chapter will show you how the performance measurement system can be placed in a larger context that will help you reap even more benefits than if it was considered a stand-alone element.

Chapter 3

The Performance Measurement System As Part of a Management System

Performance measurement is one field that has developed quite rapidly during the last few years. Comparatively, other fields such as self-assessment, benchmarking, e-business, and business process reengineering have pushed ahead in a similar fashion. While organizations must combine these and many other elements in their management approach, researchers and other scholars often seem to be so engrossed in their little sphere of the world that the potential for combination and synergy effects between such fields is not exploited fully. The fact is that performance measurement is really just one subsystem in the larger system that makes up the entire management cockpit. We started exploring this larger system in Figure 2.1, and this chapter will go further in presenting how these different subelements fit together and can reinforce each other when used correctly.

3.1 A MEASUREMENT-BASED MANAGEMENT SYSTEM

Figure 3.1 depicts our view of how a number of concepts fit together into a more coherent management system, where performance measurement and related activities are given a central role. Naturally, our view is colored by our practical experience as well as our scholarly focus, so there are certainly many different ways to look at how elements fit together. It is therefore important to point out that our purpose in presenting this model is not to stake a claim for *the* universal model of such a system, but rather to illustrate how, in fact, a number of different concepts, often viewed as isolated entities, support each other.

A more coherent management system

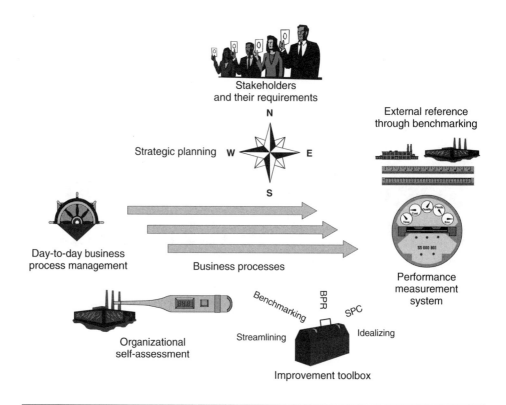

Figure 3.1   A measurement-based management system.

Three management modes: (1) strategic planning, (2) day-to-day management, (3) improvement

This model actually contains three different, but interlinked, management modes or levels: strategic planning, day-to-day management, and improvement. The rationale of the model is as follows: Together, the various stakeholders of an organization (stakeholder analysis is discussed more thoroughly in chapter 5) impose the requirements the organization must strive to fulfill in the best possible way. Strategic planning is the most important tool available to ensure that a long-term view is brought into the planning of how to meet these requirements. If we revert to the vehicle metaphor used previously, strategic planning charts the course for the organization. One ensuing challenge is to align the forces of the organization so that everyone pulls in the same direction.

This alignment is a matter of the daily management mode, and can partly be achieved by defining a sound set of business processes geared toward fulfillment of the stakeholders' needs. This is supported by the establishment of clearly communicated performance measures that direct behavior toward the strategic goals. These performance measures are used in combination with all the other "tools" available for running the daily operation. To give these measurements a reference point, performance benchmarking can be used to determine a scale for the measurement data.

Finally, the improvement mode consists of a loop of periodic application of self-assessment, improvement tools, and post-improvement follow-up through performance measurement. Self-assessment constitutes some type of diagnosis helping to identify areas of the organization in need of improvement. A multitude of different improvement tools can then be used to facilitate the required improvements, while performance measurement is used to monitor the results of the improvement efforts, to justify investments in such projects, and also to provide input into the next round of self-assessment.

Together, these three modes of management interact and reinforce each other to ensure that the activities and decisions made at the strategic level are reflected in the design of the organization, its business processes, and in the priorities set when planning activities that require improvement in order to increase the entire organization's ability to satisfy the stakeholders' needs and requirements. Whereas these linkages occur in many different ways, it is no exaggeration that the performance measurement system is one very important linking pin between these three management modes. The performance measures are an important primer for aligning the organization and its activities toward the strategic direction, they are an integral part of the daily operations management, and they are essential for tracking progress in the improvement mode.

While most of this book is dedicated to exactly this element of the model, that is, the performance measurement system and how to design it, the remainder of this chapter will be a brief journey through the other elements of the management model (except for stakeholder analysis, which is treated as part of the performance measurement system design process in chapter 5).

3.2 STRATEGIC PLANNING AND ALIGNMENT

In their study *In Search of Excellence*, Peters and Waterman (1982) emphasized strategic planning, integrated with a good understanding of your own competitive advantages, as the most important success factor. As we have already illustrated, we view strategic planning as the activity that charts the course for the organization. There are certainly more ways to view and use strategic planning, but this is probably the most common approach.

Strategic planning charts the organization's course

When it comes to the question of how strategic planning is best performed, there are probably as many answers as there are people with an opinion about the subject. We have no strong feelings about any one of the numerous approaches that are available, and we encourage you to land on a model for strategic planning that feels right and fits your organization. Later on in this book, we will venture a proposal for an approach to strategic planning that, to a higher extent than usual, incorporates performance planning into the process. This approach is presented as part of the performance measurement system design process, and is described in chapter 5.

At a low level of detail, there are basically two issues related to strategic planning:

1. Deciding on a shared view of the desired future situation and how to get there through an analysis of the organization's surroundings and own characteristics.

2. Communicating this vision throughout the organization in a manner that creates a sense of ownership and commitment, and thus ultimately results in the much-desired alignment toward this shared understanding of the future ideal. This is perhaps more important than actually reaching a plan.

A good metaphor for the alignment concept can be found in the simple physics experiments we all performed in school in order to understand the concept of magnetic force. Remember how the teacher spread many iron chips on a thin plate, with all the chips pointing in all directions? This can be compared to the employees of an organization all working without a common goal. Then, when the teacher moved the magnet underneath the plate, remember how all those chips just clicked into place at the snap of a finger? To us, this is the ideal picture of how all the parts of an organization should snap into position, perfectly aligned, when the strategic plan is communicated. We do not, of course, believe this is how it happens in real life, but it shows the meaning of alignment: to point all those chips in the same direction.

A typical planning hierarchy is often portrayed as follows:

• Vision

• Mission (purpose)

• Guiding principles (values and beliefs)

• Superordinate goals

• Goals

• Objectives

• Activities

If you have problems separating these seven different levels, time lines, and details, join the club (a club that is probably very extensive)! This might be a reasonable model in a book dealing exclusively with strategic planning, but we do not wish to go into this kind of complexity here. For our purposes, in order to integrate strategic planning into the overall management system, the plan must consist of at least:

- An overall vision of the organization's reasons for existence, that is, what it wants to achieve or what meaning it wants to have for its stakeholders

- Additionally, specific objectives defining what the organization wants to achieve at different milestones

- An outline of activities, at a rather high level, required for fulfilling the vision and attaining the objectives

Three elements of a strategic plan

The vision should be the organization's North Star, the overall ideal state it strives to reach. The time line of the vision could be up to 20 years. Many might argue that that is too long in today's world of ever-increasingly rapid cycles of change, but the point of the vision is not exact fulfillment. The main purpose is to develop a shared view of the long-term meaning of the organization to ensure consistency at the lower levels of planning. Scenarios for what will decide future success will change over time and the vision will be updated accordingly.

The vision should be the organization's North Star

Defined objectives are more specific translations of where the organization needs to move to fulfill the vision and are meant to be attained. Higher-level strategic objectives should be set ambitiously to give the organization something to reach for, but they must ultimately be possible to reach so that later cycles of strategic planning can progress to even more ambitious goals. To enable a review of the goal attainment during the previous period, these objectives should also be quantified.

These objectives are subsequently translated into strategic activities whose completion should move the organization toward attainment of the objectives and fulfillment of the vision. Such activities often become the main focus for management, since these are the tasks that will bring the organization closer to its goals and truly constitute leadership.

In general, the development of this hierarchy of different strategic elements must be based on an assessment of the following issues (and probably many more):

- Stakeholder needs and requirements

- Management ambitions

- Competitors' initiatives

- Technological development

- Financial needs

- Political decisions

- Trade regulations

- Changing legislation

- Environmental constraints

Strategic planning must involve the organization

It should also be pointed out that strategic planning traditionally has been a task for top management. There is typically little willingness to involve others in the process, which is motivated by the need for confidentiality to avoid competitors gaining any insight into the game plan for the battle. However, such confidentiality seems to confuse middle managers and other employees more than it does "the enemies." Modern strategic planning should:

- Involve more people

- Be structured but less formal

- Focus on the plan and the process

- Drive the budget

- Develop better balance between marketing, finance, and operations

- Lengthen the planning horizons

- Link action planning and effective implementation more effectively

The planning process needs to involve many more people than is usually the case. Effective implementation requires a feeling of ownership and involvement by those who are ultimately going to implement the plan. Those involved in implementation must also play a part in the development process. People in the organization have ideas and experiences that could provide valuable input to this process.

On a positive note, each level of this hierarchy of elements is a direct translation of the level above and supports its attainment. As such, these strategic elements can be further broken down into more operational factors, which is where the business processes come into play. They should ideally be designed to fulfill these strategic elements (which, in turn, are based on the stakeholders' needs and requirements). Since we have stated that the performance measurement system will measure the performance of these business processes, these measurements actually become, albeit indirectly, measurements of fulfillment of the strategic plan. This is the practical manifestation of alignment, even though it does not occur as instantly as the iron chip alignment from the magnetic force experiment.

3.3 BUSINESS PROCESSES

Over the last couple of decades, an alternative to the traditional, department-based organization has evolved—the business process view. Numerous volumes have been written that testify to the rationale for this transition and the benefits it carries, so we will not pursue this subject very far.

Organizing people and work in departments certainly provides some benefits:

- People specialize within their field of expertise, thus developing a highly refined set of skills.

- Costs are lowered by centralizing various functions, for example, finance, personnel, maintenance, and so on so that a smaller number of specialists can service the needs of many other functional areas.

- Concentrated areas of specialists will usually be quick to pick up the latest developments within that field and bring them into the organization.

- A secure workplace setting, so that everyone knows where they belong, which tasks they are supposed to perform, and what the career patterns ahead look like.

- The organization can easily be drawn and presented as a well-defined structure.

It has, however, become increasingly obvious that the contradiction between the organizational layout and the tasks the organization is supposed to execute have created several problems. As soon as people are established within a square in a departmental organization chart, it often seems as if the lines of this box become inescapable solid boundaries. Communication across the borders is kept to a minimum, and a department member will only perform tasks that naturally belong to the area of responsibility in her or his department. Each department seeks to maximize its influence and authority while at the same time optimizing the performance level within the unit. Furthermore, the focus of attention often becomes "the boss," that is, the immediate superior—not the customer. The end result is usually that the whole is far from being more than the sum of the individual elements, and in the worst case, far less. Each department suboptimizes within its area of responsibility, which in turn leads to conflicting objectives and conflicting actions between different departments. The total performance level of the organization is naturally in line with this.

Advantages of department-based organization

Why view business processes

These and many other problems have been the basis for the changes over the last few years, from viewing the company as a number of departments to focusing on the business processes being performed. Several issues make this a logical transition:

- Every process has a customer, and focusing on the process ensures better focus on the customer

- Creating value with regard to the end product takes place in horizontal processes

- Defining process boundaries and the customers and suppliers of the processes achieves better communication and well-understood requirements

- Managing entire processes running through many departments rather than managing individual departments reduces the risk of suboptimization

- Appointing so-called process owners, who are responsible for the process, avoids the traditional fragmentation of responsibility often seen in a functional organization

- Managing processes provides a better foundation for measuring and controlling performance levels

In this book, we consider an organization to consist of a set of business processes that can be service-creation processes: physical manufacturing, administrative support, management, and so on. The main point is that these processes are designed to perform specific tasks. They will often, but not necessarily, involve a number of people or even run through several departments. Since the set of business processes constituting the organization represents those activities deemed necessary to fulfill the needs and requirements of the stakeholders, managing the business through these processes ensures the desired alignment from the strategic direction down to the detailed work being completed. As such, these business processes are also the ideal units of analysis for performance measurement. The rationale is that the organization's stakeholders define the strategy, which is translated into a set of business processes required to implement it. By measuring the performance of these business processes, we provide a foundation for monitoring and improving their performance, which in turn directly transmits up to the strategy and the stakeholders' needs fulfillment.

For a more thorough treatment of which typical business processes occur in an organization, how to identify them, and how to map them, you should consult other sources, for instance *Mapping Work Processes* by Dianne Galloway (1994). In this book, we trust that you are familiar with the concept and your own business processes, and leave the subject with the conclusion that performance measurement should focus strongly on business process measurement.

3.4 BENCHMARKING

In a larger management model, such as the one depicted in Figure 3.1, benchmarking can serve at least three different purposes. These are linked to the three basic types of benchmarking that have been developed:

Types of benchmarking

1. Strategic benchmarking: learn from benchmarking partners which strategic direction to pursue, based on their previous experience.

2. Performance benchmarking: focus on comparing performance levels among the benchmarking partners.

3. Process benchmarking: go beyond the performance levels to study, understand, and learn how benchmarking partners are able to attain certain performance levels.

First of all, as a tool or input to the strategic planning process of the organization, strategic benchmarking can be used to gain inspiration and ideas. There are a great many organizations out there, and although many like to think of themselves as highly unique, very few actually are. When you are faced with important decisions about which competitive strategy to pursue, which technology to go with, which markets to serve, and so on, chances are somebody else has faced a similar decision and researched it to such an extent that you can benefit from his experience. Still, it should be said that strategic benchmarking can be difficult, not the least of which is identifying relevant, good, and willing benchmarking partners.

Strategic benchmarking

Secondly, performance benchmarking can function as a performance measurement reference scale, as previously explained. Since all the internal performance measurement in an organization will always be only relative, that is, the measurement levels themselves say nothing much about how well they compare with external standards, they can only provide data to trace the trend. This is not completely true, since some types of relative measures have more meaning than merely trend development, for example, customer satisfaction, delivery completeness, and inventory turnover rate. For such measures, there are more or less established standards for what is bad, good, or excellent. Where this is not intuitive,

Performance benchmarking

benchmarking can provide an objective reference that makes it possible to judge whether a certain performance level is acceptable, excellent, average, or in need of improvement.

Process benchmarking

Finally, process benchmarking, which is typically an improvement-oriented approach, naturally belongs in the improvement toolbox. This involves seeking ideas and inspiration as to how business processes can be redesigned for improved performance from benchmarking partners that have excelled at these processes. This is the most widely used type of benchmarking and is well documented in a number of good publications. Thus, we will not discuss in this book how to undertake a process benchmarking study. It is one of several tools in the improvement toolbox, and will not be treated differently from the others, but some overall guidelines to this toolbox are presented at the end of this chapter.

3.5 DAY-TO-DAY BUSINESS MANAGEMENT

Although this is a topic we could have dedicated an entire book to, the purpose of this chapter is merely to illustrate how your performance measurement system fits into a larger picture. Thus, we will not spend much time discussing the management of your business in everyday life.

How management spends its time

We prefer to draw your attention to an area that we feel quite strongly about—how management spends its time. First of all, there is a difference between what is often termed *management*, the operational attention to getting the job done from day to day, and *leadership*, which keeps a long-term view on the course followed by the organization. It is interesting to see how management typically divides its time between these two concepts (in fact, there is a third, firefighting, which we feel is a waste of time). If we break this down even further, management time could be divided into the three groups suggested in Figure 3.2.

Catering for crises creates heroes of the organization

Such a division of three equal parts is certainly not a realistic picture for most companies. Catering for crises is probably the dominating task for most managers. Many companies have an organizational culture where the "firefighters" are the heroes. Their style is vigorous and results-oriented, which matches the Western management ideal perfectly. However, these "firefighters" often represent the short-term focus that is detrimental to many organizations. Short-term solutions in an environment characterized by rapid change may, on the surface, look appropriate. Short-term solutions to crises could, however, direct the organization to more or less incidental solutions that are actually inefficient and expensive. In our opinion, this portion of management's time is neither management nor leadership, but

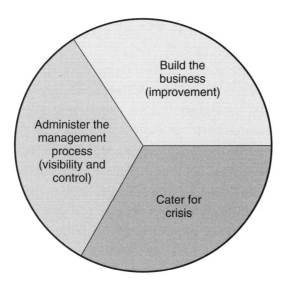

Figure 3.2 How management spends its time.

rather a waste of time that could have been avoided (or at least minimized) in the presence of true management and leadership.

Management

Management, in the sense of making sure that the right things are done the right way, that your subordinates are comfortable in their work environment, and so on, should be about half of any manager's job. These are the activities that may seem boring or less inspiring than other ways of spending your time, but are really needed to keep the business processes running smoothly. Properly exerted day-to-day management will keep the crises at bay and free up time for the more proactive leadership.

Leadership

In a rapidly changing environment, a more effective survival strategy than firefighting is developing true ability for organizational change. Continuously building on and expanding the competence base of the organization, introducing tools and approaches for improvement, initiating improvement projects, and generally thinking ahead so that the organization literally teems with excitement and improvement efforts are the core building blocks of operational leadership. In organizations where the crises are increasing in frequency and seriousness, there is usually too little attention paid to this type of leadership and business improvement. This steals so much time that even less is done in the way of business building, which not surprisingly adds to the crisis level, and thus the evil cycle spirals further. Freeing up time for leadership is challenging, but pays off tenfold. Fortunately, a state-of-the-art performance measurement system supports both management and leadership by providing real-time and operational data for making decisions, and also has the ability to create the organizationwide motivation necessary to achieve an organization teeming with such improvement activities.

3.6 SELF-ASSESSMENT

Self-assessment is a technique for evaluating the performance level of an organization and its processes. The word *self* separates the evaluation from those conducted by an external third party, that is, the organization performs the evaluation itself, unlike assessments made during certification, supplier evaluation, or for quality awards. From this definition, self-assessment sounds much like an ordinary performance measurement system. What, then, separates a "normal" performance measurement system from self-assessment? The line is not crystal clear, but in our opinion there are a number of main differences that justify including both self-assessment and the performance measurement system in the overall management system we have outlined.

The first difference is the frequency of measurement. Whereas your state-of-the-art performance measurement system will perform continuous measurement of the organization, self-assessment is conducted at certain intervals, usually every 6 or 12 months. The focus of measurement is the second difference. While the performance measurement system provides detailed measurements for every single business process, the purpose of self-assessment is to give an overall and more coherent picture of the organization's performance. Thus, self-assessment is not intended to be the instrument panel attached to every business process, but more of a helicopter view of the entire organization. This is linked to the third main difference, the use of the assessments or measurements. Data from the performance measurement system is used mainly for the day-to-day running of the processes and monitoring of improvements. Self-assessment results are used to a much larger degree for defining more long-term focus areas for improvement and as strategic decision support. The fourth (and final) main difference lies in the execution of the measurements. One feature of your state-of-the-art performance measurement system is that it collects the performance data as automatically as possible and presents it to the users. When a self-assessment is conducted, people typically have to manually collect data, sort them, and make them presentable for further analysis and use.

In summary, measurement by self-assessment is performed at a more coherent and overall strategic level and is conducted at a lower frequency. We would also like to point out that there are, in fact, different types of self-assessment. During recent years, many organizations have started conducting self-assessments based on the criteria of quality awards such as The Malcolm Baldrige National Quality Award, and the European Quality Award from the European Foundation for Quality Management.

The criteria for evaluation in these awards are more or less defined along process-independent dimensions. Another approach builds on measurements at the business process level, and in these cases the approach is tailored to a single organization.

It is also important to maintain the organization's self-assessment approach, both to keep and even to improve its ability to conduct correct and valuable assessments. The need for adjustments to the system arises as a consequence of experience from using self-assessment, as well as changing conditions surrounding the organization. Maintenance consists of a more defensive adjustment of the system parts that are obviously obsolete, for example, removing processes that are no longer performed by the organization. Of greater importance is a proactive development of the system to give even more valuable information, that is, changing the focus of the measurements to areas expected to become more vital in the future. There is, however, a potential conflict between the desire for changing the system and the need for stability of the measures used. Without a certain degree of continuity, comparisons against previous measurements will prove meaningless.

3.7 IMPROVEMENT TOOLBOX

If you go to the trouble of trying to identify every improvement tool that has been designed (as we indeed have), you will soon realize that there are many different tools that could belong in the improvement toolbox.

Do not focus on the tools for the sake of the tools

A paradox about a toolbox is that while it contains a large number of tools, the tools themselves should not be the focus of attention. It is inherent in the nature of tools that their purpose is to offer support. Wanting to fix a car, the tools that will work to get the job done are selected and used. The desired result is a car that runs, and it is of no importance whether a wrench, pliers, or a screwdriver was used. Similarly, the desired results for organizations are improved performance and competitiveness. For this purpose, they can use whatever tools fit as long as they give results. It is thus far more important to know how to select the right tool and use it to reach the set goals than to know a large number of different tools.

All the tools in the improvement toolbox should therefore be regarded as belonging to a large, well-equipped toolbox available for the organization striving to improve. They should supplement each other and function in symbiosis. Which tool is used in a specific situation is dependent upon characteristics of the organization using it and the situation in which it is applied. First, the situation and problem at hand must be defined, then a

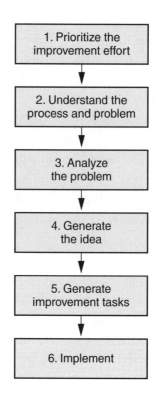

Figure 3.3 Different stages in a general business process improvement project.

A business process improvement process

suitable tool must be selected to improve it. If you only have one tool, say a hammer, it is amazing how quickly all problems begin to look like nails.

We urge organizations to get acquainted with a number of different tools. It is not necessary to know *all* the tools, but it is advantageous to know a *good selection* of them. This enables you to be flexible in applying tools. Each tool has its strengths and weaknesses, so it is important to select the right tool for the problem, not the other way around.

We will close this chapter by looking briefly at a classification of what we consider to be prominent tools in the improvement toolbox. Figure 3.3 shows a generic process of six stages that should be accomplished in a general business process improvement project. These phases should seem logical: running through a sequence of stages to select the problem to solve, understanding and analyzing this problem, generating improvement ideas and tasks, and implementing the improved solution. For each of these stages, there are a number of tools available (and some are even applicable in more than one stage), and it is quite helpful to categorize the tools according to which stage they primarily belong to.

Tools that can assist the task of prioritizing the improvement effort by analyzing which business processes or areas of the organization are in need of improvement are:

- Self-assessment, to form an overall impression of the organization's performance level. While self-assessment is presented as a tool in the improvement toolbox, it is also a more comprehensive concept, as described in the previous section.

- Trend analysis, to evaluate the development of the organization's performance level in the aftermath of a self-assessment.

Trend analysis, scatter charts, and performance matrices are treated in more detail in chapter 13

- Spider chart, to compare an organization's performance level against other similar organizations.

- Performance matrix, where the objective is to analyze the different business processes' need for improvement based on their importance and current performance level.

- Criteria testing, which is a numerical tool for analyzing which business processes have the highest impact on the critical success factors of the organization.

- Quality function deployment (QFD), which in this context is used to coherently plan an organization's improvement activities by considering both external requirements and demands posed by the strategy. This is explained in more detail in chapter 6.

After deciding which business process should be improved, the next logical step is to document and understand the process, both on a deeper level and with regard to more detailed problems within the process. Tools for this purpose are:

- Relationship mapping, a high-level mapping tool used to produce an initial picture of which stakeholders and employees are involved in a certain process, as well as the relationships between them

- Flowchart , perhaps one of the most classic tools ever devised, used in a large variety of situations to draw detailed charts of business processes or other sequences of activities

- Critical incident, which is a technique for identifying problems within an area or process based on determining the occurrences that cause the most severe problems

- Check sheet, which is used for collecting data about a process or problem area through systematic recording in a predefined table

- Pareto chart, the classic chart used to sort problems or causes according to importance, based on the so-called 80/20 rule

Pareto chart is treated in more detail in chapter 13

Another essential stage in the improvement work is problem analysis. Some tools in this category are:

- Cause-and-effect chart, often called the fishbone chart, to identify causes of a problem by systematically running through a tree chart structure

- Root cause analysis, also called the why–why chart, to delve deeply into the root causes of a problem

- Scatter chart, to detect correlations between phenomena

- Histogram, to sort data about a process in a clear manner for visual study of patterns

- Relations diagram, to help identify links between effects and their probable causes

- Matrix diagram, to graphically portray data and see connections and relations

In the stage for idea generation, there are again several tools:

- Brainstorming, the most basic of these techniques, where the intent is to create as many ideas as possible

- Brainwriting/Crawford slip method, which is similar to a written version of brainstorming

- Nominal group technique, which is a formal way of generating ideas

- Affinity chart, which is a way to organize thoughts or ideas based on some kind of connection between them

Pure improvement tools, that is, tools whose main purpose is to achieve improvements, include:

- Streamlining, which is a collective term for several principles to simplify business processes, eliminate waste, and increase efficiency

- Idealizing, used to find the ideal process when disregarding practical limitations

- Quality function deployment (QFD), potentially combined with a system diagram, in this context to design products or processes based on customer requirements.

- Work unit analysis, to analyze the customer/supplier relationship between segments of a business process to improve the interfaces between them.

- Statistical process control, to monitor processes through the use of control charts.

- Business process reengineering (BPR), one of the "hotter" tools lately. The core of BPR is to completely rebuild a process to achieve dramatic performance improvements.

- Benchmarking, which seeks to create improvements through learning from other organizations.

A last group contains tools or techniques aimed at planning the implementation of and setting targets for improvements:

- Tree diagram, to plan a project, for example an improvement implementation.

- Process decision program chart, to prevent undesirable events from occurring.

- AΔT analysis, to set ambitious targets for the improvement activity.

- Force field analysis, to identify forces working for and against an implementation of improvements.

Let us reiterate that perhaps the most important issue when dealing with this improvement toolbox is to understand which tool to apply in a given situation. Unfortunately, there are no guidelines for this decision, because it is too complex to describe in an easily presentable manner. But Table 3.1 presents some data regarding typical resource requirements needed for the selection of tools.

An indication of resource needs when applying different tools in the improvement toolbox

This concludes the chapters of an introductory nature. The next chapter introduces the process for designing and implementing your state-of-the-art performance measurement system. The rest of the book will take you through each phase of that process in detail.

Table 3.1   Resource requirements for different tools.

Resource Requirements	Prioritizing	Problem Understanding	Problem Analysis	Idea Generation	Improvement Proposals	Implemen-tation
Less resources required	Trend analysis	Critical incident	Cause-and-effect chart	Brain-storming	Idealizing	Tree diagram
	Performance matrix	Check sheet	Root cause analysis	Brainwriting		PDPC
	Spider chart	Pareto chart	Scatter chart	Crawford slip method		AΔT analysis
	Criteria testing		Histogram	Nominal group technique		Force field analysis
			Relations diagram	Affinity chart		
			Matrix diagram			
Medium resources required	QFD	Relationship mapping			Streamlining	
		Flowchart			QFD	
					Statistical process control	
					Work unit analysis	
Many resources required	Self-assessment				Business process reengineering	
					Benchmarking	

Chapter 4

Performance Measurement System Design

We have already taken you through a brief history of performance measurement and how productivity evolved into the concept of performance. We will investigate some requirements for modern performance measurement systems before outlining a process to design your state-of-the-art performance measurement system.

4.1 REQUIREMENTS FOR MODERN PERFORMANCE MEASUREMENT SYSTEMS

Just as performance measurement (or, previously, productivity measurement) has been based on financial figures, traditional performance measurement systems were based on management accounting systems and primarily concerned with cost. In today's business environment, however, accounting-based performance measurement systems are no longer sufficient. The new performance measurement systems required by world-class enterprises must (Maskell 1991; Kaydos 1998):

Accounting-based performance measurement systems are no longer sufficient

- Be directly related to the enterprise's strategy, to link the measurements made to the overall course of the organization.

Characteristics of modern performance measurement systems

- Provide "wholeness," that is, they must contain all the variables required to define "good performance."

- Primarily use nonfinancial measures, as most aspects of performance for a modern organization stem from dimensions other than finance.

- Vary between locations since different parts of the organization have different needs. A truly powerful performance measurement system will allow customization.

- Change over time as needs change; a static performance measurement system will quickly become obsolete.

- Be simple and easy to use. The time has passed when performance measurement systems were so complex that only the most ardent users could understand them.

- Provide fast feedback to operators and managers. Lagging and outdated measures are of little use in a world where speed is constantly increasing.

- Be accurate, if not in absolute terms, at least in terms of producing consistency of error. For the sake of improvement, consistency is normally more important than absolute accuracy, as we are looking for changes in levels.

- Be intended to foster improvement rather than simply monitor performance.

- Be able to explain the gap between current and desired performance by breaking the gap down into components that can be addressed.

- Provide sufficient detail to be able to pinpoint where action should be taken, but they should also be able to present enough high-level information so that a quick overview can be gained.

- Promote absence of fear, one of Deming's fourteen points (Deming, 1996), which clearly applies to performance measurement systems. For a system to work and not be sabotaged or have data distorted on purpose, there must be no fear of being punished for poor performance.

- Enable accountability, that is, place the responsibility for both good and bad performance where it belongs to avoid situations where no one takes the initiative to correct situations when they are to blame.

This is a very extensive list of requirements, probably enough to make anyone think twice about trying to design a performance measurement system! The purpose of presenting this list is not, however, to define such high expectations that you think you could never succeed. Rather, this list serves as a checklist for issues to keep in mind when developing you own performance measurement system, presented in full confidence that rarely has any performance measurement system fulfilled every one of these require-ments. Designing *and* implementing a state-of-the-art performance mea-surement system is a process that could take years and years of fine-tuning before you get where you really want to be. Our advice is to start with the basics: get a system up and running that measures the most important aspects of performance that you would like to measure, that seems to be sufficiently accurate, and that is actually being used. Then you can start tweaking it to fulfill the other requirements. This is also reflected in the per-formance measurement system design strategy presented next.

4.2 PERFORMANCE MEASUREMENT SYSTEM DESIGN STRATEGY

When designing and implementing a performance measurement system, the resulting system will become part of and impact the working life of most of the employees in the organization. Thus, the approach taken to designing and implementing the system will greatly affect the extent to which it is accepted, appreciated, and used by those people for whom it was intended. There are certainly a number of ways you could go about this process, but a useful distinction, albeit perhaps somewhat old-fashioned, is between:

- A top-down cascading method

- A bottom-up design process

Two performance measurement system design approaches

These two approaches represent extremes when it comes to the level of involvement of the regular employee in the design process, and they both display inherent strengths and weaknesses. By merging the two approaches, it is possible to combine their strengths and hopefully avoid some of their weaknesses.

The top-down cascading approach, whether it is used for strategic planning, defining objectives, or designing a performance measurement system, is perhaps the most widespread approach. The rationale of the approach is that top management knows best which strategy to follow, which objectives to strive for, or what aspects of performance to measure. Thus, the process begins with a definition of the higher-level issues, for example, the top-level performance indicators to be measured and followed. These top-level indicators are then broken down into increasingly more detailed indicators via a cascading process through the formal organiza-tional hierarchy. The formal manager/subordinate relationship is the main transfer link for this approach, and the result is, as the name clearly

The top-down cascading approach

implies, a performance measurement system dictated and derived from top management's perceptions of what is important to measure.

Advantages of the top-down cascading approach

The advantage of this approach is that the alignment discussed previously (see Figure 3.1) is quite easy to achieve, at least in theory. Since performance indicators at all levels of the organization are derived from the top-level indicators, which in turn are linked to the strategic thinking of top management, they all reflect and support the course charted for the organization. This aspect is also pivotal to maintain in a combination approach to performance measurement system design.

Challenges of the top-down cascading approach

The main challenge in the top-down cascading approach is to obtain buy-in and acceptance from the employees of the organization. Since the system is being designed from the top and "forced" onto the organization, it is easy to see why there might be problems with people not accepting the system, not believing it will measure what they think is important, or rejecting it simply because they were left out of the design process. Some generally accepted ways to alleviate this problem are: explain to the entire organization the motivation and thinking behind the design of the performance measurement system; encourage its use rather than prescribing it; describe the system in a way that the entire organization understands; and define the right for each level of the organization to question the validity of its indicators.

Advantages of the bottom-up approach

A bottom-up process, on the other hand, is based on personal responsibility and is well-suited for designing a performance measurement system that every member of the organization feels ownership of, can relate to, and generally views as useful. In this approach, every employee is responsible for contributing to the definition of performance indicators covering their process or area. Upward throughout the organization, the individual indicators are then merged through accumulating the measurements, combining them through some arithmetic operations, or putting them together into a large report. The resulting performance measurement system will normally be perceived as useful at the individual business process level, as the performance indicators have been tailored to the needs of those working in

Problems with the bottom-up approach

that process. However, what the system has gained in terms of organizational acceptance can often be lost in terms of coherency and the desired alignment toward shared goals and a joint strategic direction.

There are several ways of combining these two approaches. One method we witnessed first-hand was to complete both approaches simultaneously, all the way through to a final measurement system, and then the one that seemed better was selected by a democratic vote to ensure acceptance. However, this is very resource-intensive and rarely results in a generally accepted system anyway.

A combined approach

What we encourage is a slightly different way of combining the top-down and bottom-up strategies. In our experience, the most successful way is to let these two approaches meet somewhere in the middle. To achieve alignment of the defined performance measures and the longer-term strategic direction of the organization, the strategy should be used to define the coarse direction of the performance measurement system at all levels of the organization. For example, if the strategy involves improved customer satisfaction through shorter servicing times, then this should be a basic foundation for the entire performance measurement system, thus leading to a number of different performance measures that push the organization toward reduced servicing times. However, instead of mechanically converting this higher-level strategic direction into simple permutations of lower-level performance indicators, the organization should be allowed the freedom to define these as they see fit. The employees of the organization are those that will use the performance measurement system from day to day, and they know best which detailed performance measures will work better for them. Thus, as long as they stay within the rough boundaries of the overall strategic course chartered by top management, they should be able to define these lower-level measures. Since this approach can introduce inconsistencies and conflicting measures, running through a design process stage where such inconsistencies are eliminated can counter any negative effects.

This combination approach both ensures that the organization's guiding star—its strategy—defines the boundaries for the performance measurement system and simultaneously encourages ownership and use of the system by allowing the users to define the details of the system themselves. We also feel confident that there are other combination approaches that could work equally well.

Finally, before we proceed to the design process, let us also clarify our position regarding the level of measurement within the organization. Now and then, in both our work and projects we have been involved in, we run into discussions about how low you should go in terms of measuring activity in the organization. Some argue that performance measurement can be carried out even at the individual employee level. This subject is also touched upon elsewhere in this book, but to summarize, we feel that you should avoid such measurements as much as possible. In some cases, they can be useful and are often applied to salespeople or others working in a bonus pay system. Still, we have found very few cases where such a fine-toothed measurement system is needed and adds additional benefits beyond the business process, department, or team level. On the contrary, there are many examples of cases where individual performance measurement does more harm than good. Not only does it require much effort to be able to measure at such a high level of detail, but measurements can be abused and people generally feel uneasy about them. The main problems include:

Problems with performance measurement at the individual employee level

- The type of performance measurement that enables achieved performance levels to be attributed to individual employees' actions (or lack thereof) is often considered threatening by those subjected to such measurement.

- Once performance data are available, it is easy to fall for the temptation of using the measurements for punishment or reprimand, which will very quickly destroy all trust people might have had in the performance measurement system and make it virtually useless in the future.

- Measuring at such a high level of organizational detail naturally requires more performance data, resulting in more extensive performance reports, requiring more storage space, and so on. Typically, this makes the entire system explode in terms of data collection effort, storage capacity, data management requirements, and so on.

- A performance measurement system is capable of altering the behavior of people, as previously discussed. This is especially true when measuring the performance of individuals and can lead to very unfortunate examples of suboptimization. This is illustrated in two examples following.

Two particular situations come to mind where we have seen individual-level measurement create undesired behavior. Several years ago we worked with a company that produced a large variety of fishing hooks. Many were created from the same basic molded piece of metal, but were turned into a large number of different variants by painting them in different patterns and affixing different types of feathers, hooks, and so on, to them. The manufacturing department was laid out such that the molded pieces were placed in a large storage bin in front of a number of parallel stations doing the painting and assembly of different types of hooks. At some point, the company introduced a payment system where the line operators were paid according to how many hooks they pushed through the system. They soon saw one of the effects of this system, namely that the bin of molded pieces was emptied several times during the day while the finished goods inventory at the other end was building rapidly. The competition among the operators to push through as many hooks as possible made them produce far more hooks than there were orders for, thus depleting the raw material inventory. If, instead, the company had measured the degree of order fulfillment for the entire production department, this situation would have been avoided.

The other example is not from a company we have worked with, but rather one we were customers of quite recently. After traveling for nearly

24 hours, we arrived at a hotel where we were supposed to stay for a few days. The time was around 2 PM, and we were told no rooms were yet ready for us, we would have to wait until 4 PM. In spite of being less than happy about the wait, tired as we were, we could not help but make some observations as we watched how the chambermaids and the reception clerk proceeded during the next couple of hours. The very apologetic check-in clerk clearly tried to make the chambermaids hurry up and get two rooms ready sooner, while they were obviously dragging their feet and seriously procrastinating. As the afternoon wore on, we came to understand why. It turned out that the hotel had a system in place where the chambermaids were assigned one room at a time and had to report back to management after each completed room to get the next assignment. If they ran out of rooms to clean before they finished their shift at 4 PM, they were either assigned to even less popular jobs, for instance sweeping cigarette butts in the parking lot, or they were dismissed for the day. The beauty of the system lay in the fact that if the chambermaids were dismissed early since there were no more jobs for them, they only got paid for the time they had worked that day. Aside from the fact that this system demonstrated a complete lack of respect for these employees, it was also the obvious reason why few rooms were ever ready before close to 4 PM.

4.3 THE PERFORMANCE MEASUREMENT SYSTEM DESIGN PROCESS

Finally, we have arrived at the actual performance measurement system design process. We present an eight-step process that we have designed based on our experiences working with a number of organizations in performance measurement system design projects. However, as we have tried to emphasize a few times already, we are not in any way fanatical about the concepts and approaches put forward in this book. Being confident that there are a dozen different ways of successfully designing your state-of-the-art performance measurement system, we hope you will merely view this process as one suggested and possible way of accomplishing this task.

An eight-step design process

Our performance measurement system design process is illustrated in Figure 4.1.

The process runs through eight steps, and each of the ensuing chapters deals with one of these steps in greater detail. The remainder of this chapter will very briefly outline the contents of these eight steps and explain the rationale for the design of this process.

Before this process is even started with Step 1, the organization must establish a core team that will carry the performance measurement system

Figure 4.1   The performance measurement system design process.

design process forward. In the previous section, we argued that a combination of the top-down cascading and bottom-up approaches is preferable, but there still needs to be a core team in charge of the design process. In our experience, this team should be broadly composed, including representatives from both top and middle management and regular employees. It should not be too large, normally not more than four or five members; the broad masses of people in the organization will have their say during the various steps of the design process, when the bottom-up approach for populating the performance measurement system with detailed performance indicators is started. We could also devote several pages to telling you that this team must have a clear mandate, clear objectives, and a clear progress plan to work by, but this so obviously applies to any type of development project that we will spare you the details of these issues.

As for the duration of and resource investments in a typical performance measurement system design project, such figures are as easy to present with any accuracy as estimating how long it will take the average reader to read this book from start to finish—it is impossible. These figures vary so much from organization to organization that any attempt would be mere guesswork. However, what we can tell you is that we have never seen anyone design and implement a performance measurement system in less than four months, and it has never, in any of the cases we have worked with, taken more than one year to arrive at a version of a system that can claim to be working. As we will explain later on, a performance measurement system is never finished, it is a dynamic and living entity for its entire lifetime, but it should not take more than a year to have something in place that is up and running. A typical trait is also that the larger the organization, the longer it takes to design and implement the system. And, of course, the project duration depends on the "fancy level" of the system; a completely computerized, Web-based, and customizable system will take longer to produce than a simple paper-based one.

Turning to the question of resources invested in such systems, providing an answer becomes even more impossible. Depending on how much of the work is carried out using internal resources as opposed to hired consultants, the complexity of the system, the amount of background data already available, and so on, the costs can range from almost nothing for copying pre-existing reports to probably a million dollars for a first-class system.

Briefly, the eight steps of the design process are:

1. *Understanding and mapping business structures and processes.* This is the introductory step of the design process, whose main purpose is to force those setting out to design a performance measurement system to think through and reacquaint themselves with the organization, its

Step 1: Understanding and mapping business structures and processes

competitive position, the environment it exists in, and, not in the least, its business processes. This might seem like a superfluous task, since it is obvious that the people of the organization live and breathe these issues every day. Experience shows that this is not the case! After having been taken through an exercise like this, most managers agree that they are normally so entrenched in day-to-day operational issues that such an effort is not only a welcome break, but also an opportunity to revisit some of the strategic issues of the organization. As such, this step nicely lays the foundation for proceeding with the design process, having the basic business understanding fresh in the minds of the design team.

Step 2: Developing business performance priorities

2. *Developing business performance priorities.* This step aligns with the earlier argument that the performance measurement system should be a consequence of and support the chain of stakeholders' requirements from the organization's strategy through to its business processes—which are designed to satisfy the stakeholders' requirements. To accomplish the match between this chain and the performance measurement system, this order of priorities must be in place well before the design process enters into the actual design phases. If these priorities have not been previously developed and articulated, this is an ideal time to accomplish what any organization should already have established. If these priorities are in place, then a quick revision is a useful way to go through this step.

Step 3: Understanding the current performance measurement system

3. *Understanding the current performance measurement system.* Even if you don't call it a performance measurement system, every organization has some kind of measurement system in place already. Building on this assumption, there are basically two ways of approaching the design and implementation of a new performance measurement system. Either you scrap the old system and introduce the new one as a replacement, or you redevelop the existing into the new system. Both can certainly work, but we have seen many examples of the former approach leading to trouble. People will cling to the old measurement system and either use both in parallel or actually use the old one and simply go through the motions with the new one. Naturally, this is a very undesirable outcome after having spent resources to develop a new performance measurement system. This outcome is eliminated by taking the latter approach, but this can also introduce some additional challenges before you end up with your ideal measurement system. We still recommend this approach, though, and understanding the current system is therefore a logical step in the design process.

Step 4: Developing performance indicators

4. *Developing performance indicators.* The most important element of your state-of-the-art performance measurement system is the set of performance indicators you will use to measure your organization's performance

and business processes. This is the point in the design process where the top-down cascading approach meets the bottom-up design approach and where the broad masses of the organization become involved. As the name implies, the purpose of this step is to develop the performance measurement system with an appropriate amount of relevant and precise performance indicators. This is somewhat of a science in its own right, and chapter 8 will take you through this in detail.

5. *Deciding how to collect the required data.* This step is closely linked with the preceding performance indicator definition step. Developing all those perfect performance indicators that will tell you everything you ever wanted to know about what goes on in your organization is one thing, but being able to collect the data required to calculate these performance indicators is a completely different matter. This issue must initially be addressed during the development of the performance indicators to avoid those that can never actually be measured. But this is also an essential step, the main purpose of which is to arrive at solutions for collecting the necessary data for the final, defined indicators. Although accountants used to play a prominent role in this step, the proliferation of modern enterprise resource planning (ERP) systems has turned this into more of an exercise of figuring out which data can be extracted from the data warehouses of these systems. The evolution toward so-called automated performance measurement systems will be discussed in chapter 9.

Step 5: Deciding how to collect the required data

6. *Designing reporting and performance data presentation formats.* This step is somewhat connected to the data collection question of the previous step, but goes much further. In this step, you will decide how the performance data will be presented to the users; how they should apply the performance data for management, monitoring, and improvement; who will have access rights to performance data, and so on. To some extent, this can be compared to the design of the dashboard in a car, where you have to make judgments regarding ergonomic considerations, the human mind's abilities for perception and data interpretation, and application of the performance data by managers and employees. The end result of this step should be a performance measurement system that has found its place in the overall measurement-based management system presented in Figure 3.1.

Step 6: Designing reporting and performance data presentation formats

7. *Testing and adjusting the performance measurement system.* We have already warned you that your first pass at the performance measurement system will not be completely right—there are bound to be performance indicators that do not work as intended, conflicting indicators, undesired behavior, problems with data availability, and so on. This is to be expected

Step 7: Testing and adjusting the performance measurement system

and is perfectly normal; in this step you will undertake extensive testing of the system and adjust elements that do not work as planned. The result is a system where the main and most obvious quirks have been eliminated, but it would still be naïve to believe that the system is perfect. Rather, a performance measurement system should be construed as a never-ending journey toward perfection. The environment of the system will change, the organization and its needs will be altered, and the performance measurement system itself will constantly transform, both to accommodate these changes and to eliminate further design problems. However, at the end of this step, major problems should have been identified and eliminated to allow full-blown implementation of the system.

*Step 8:
Implementing the
performance
measurement system*

8. *Implementing the performance measurement system.* In the last step of the performance measurement system design process, the system is finally implemented—put to official use. The entire process up to now has designed and, more or less, implemented the system, but this is the point where the system is officially in place and all users are given access to and can start using it. This will involve issues such as user access management, training, demonstrating that the system is important and will be used, living by the principles of the system, and so on. This step can be a lengthy one to accomplish or it can be done almost by the touch of a button.

Again, the following eight chapters will deal with each of these steps in more detail.

We should also point out that this design process, as presented here, might not be suitable for verbatim application to all types of organizations. As you will see from the following case study, the implementation we have decided to include here stems from a medium-sized organization of 300+ employees. The process outlined in this book is perfect for this size of an organization, that is, 50–1000 people.

For very small organizations, typically with less than 50 people, this process will probably seem somewhat bureaucratic. In such cases, we suggest that the design process be organized as a less extensive project driven by a small design team and that it be simplified to avoid a potential overkill of effort. Since we have been able to observe the implementation of a performance measurement system in a couple of smaller organizations, our recommendations for a simplified design process are as follows:

- Steps 1 and 2, for creating a new awareness and insight into the organization and its interactions with the environment, followed by a definition of performance priorities, can usually be combined and significantly simplified. Some of the aids described later in this book for conducting these two steps are more complex than necessary for smaller organizations, both because involvement and ownership are easier to create with fewer people, and because it is generally easier to maintain an overview of smaller organizations.

- Step 3, reviewing the existing performance measurement system, can often be skipped completely because such systems are quite rare in organizations of less than 50 people.

- Step 4, defining performance indicators, is the one step of the process that should be carried out the same way in all organizations, regardless of size. It is a very important step and being a small organization does not make it any easier to accomplish.

- Steps 5 and 6, for creating mechanisms for both performance data collection and presentation to the users, can normally be merged and simplified. This is a simpler task for smaller organizations because of the lesser amount of performance data required, the relative ease in locating the data, and the fewer number of users.

- Steps 7 and 8, for testing, adjusting, and implementing the system, are usually easier to undertake in smaller organizations and can normally be merged into one step. Again, the lesser extent of the system and fewer users make the testing and required training task less complex than in larger organizations.

At the other extreme, large organizations of more than 1000 people and typically divided into different business units or other rather autonomous entities, the process might not be able to capture the complex web of objectives, links between units, and so on that will exist. In these cases, it is usually wise to apply the performance measurement system design process to the independent business unit level first and then try to aggregate upward. This last aggregation phase will typically be geared toward uncovering conflicting objectives or performance indicators between the business units, as well as establishing the dashboard needed by corporate management to maneuver the entire organization.

A last remark about this eight-step design process; we have not outlined this process with the aim of "laying down the law." It is not an absolute process that requires being followed to the letter to work. In some cases, one or more steps may be superfluous or may not fit very well, in others there will be a need for additional tasks. Since you know your own organization far better than we do, we encourage you to make adjustments to the process to maximize the probability for success of the resulting system.

4.4 PERFORMANCE MEASUREMENT SYSTEM DESIGN CASE STUDY—PEOPLE'S BANK & INSURANCE, INTERNAL IT INFRASTRUCTURE MANAGEMENT (PBI, I³M)

Throughout the next eight chapters, the performance measurement system design process will be illustrated by means of a case study of a company we recently worked with as they designed and implemented a state-of-the-art performance measurement system. The name and type of organization has been changed, but this should have no bearing on the case's ability to enrich the tour through the design process.

People's Bank & Insurance is a large conglomerate of some 20 different companies covering a wide range of financial and insurance-related services. It started out as two separate companies—a bank and an insurance company—almost 100 years ago. About a decade ago, these two were merged "to harvest synergy effects and cover a wider range of services." As both banking and insurance have become increasingly specialized during the last few years, People's Bank & Insurance has basically become a holding company that has spawned more than 20 independent enterprises, most of them wholly owned by PBI. A small number of these independent companies have been set up to handle common services for the entire group of companies within PBI, for example, training, property management, and IT infrastructure management. PBI, I³M was founded for this latter purpose, that is, implementing, running, upgrading, and developing the IT infrastructure, both hardware and software, for the collective group of companies within PBI.

Today, four years after its inception, PBI, I³M is an organization with more than 300 employees and an annual income of about 60 million dollars. Most of the income stems from internal customers within the PBI group, but last year PBI, I³M also entered into IT infrastructure management contracts with external clients as well. The combined pressure from the PBI group to stay efficient and keep the IT infrastructure management costs as low as possible, from external customers to provide reliable services, from employees to provide better quality of work life, and from authorities regarding data security, made the company realize it needed a performance measurement system. Incidentally, at the same time, a decision was looming to process-orient the organization, and these two objectives were merged into one project termed "PBI, I³M Business Excellence." Along with the run-through of the performance measurement system design process, we will take you through PBI, I³M's efforts to design their performance measurement system in order to give you better insight into some of the issues such a project involves.

Chapter 5

Step 1: Understanding and Mapping Business Structures and Processes

STEP 1
Understanding and Mapping Business Structures and Processes

STEP 2
Developing Business Performance Priorities

STEP 3
Understanding the Current Performance Measurement System

STEP 4
Developing Performance Indicators

STEP 5
Deciding How to Collect the Required Data

STEP 6
Designing Reporting and Performance Data Presentation Formats

STEP 7
Testing and Adjusting the Performance Measurement System

STEP 8
Implementing the Performance Measurement System

As you will remember from the introduction to the design process, this first step should build the basis for the ensuing design process by thinking through and bringing up to a high level of consciousness the overall issues of the organization, its competitive position, the environment it exists in, and its business processes. There are numerous different analysis approaches that can be utilized to accomplish this step, for example, competitor analysis, value chain modeling, the stakeholder model, market and market share analysis, and enterprise modeling. Most of these, and probably many others, will normally serve the purpose of supporting this analysis. We have successfully applied one set of approaches that will be presented in this chapter.

This set of approaches spans the following sequence of steps and tools:

• Clarification of the organization's strategy, as it both defines and is shaped by the organization's stakeholders.

• Stakeholder analysis, a not-too-formal exercise that forces the design team to systematically identify and understand the people in the organization's environment that have a vested interest in the organization and its well-being—typically customers, suppliers, competitors, partners, authorities, and so on. This step culminates in a mapping of the stakeholders' expectations and requirements for the products or services delivered by the organization.

• Business process identification, a task that should produce a set of the business processes needed to satisfy the mapped stakeholder requirements representing the overall needs that the organization must fulfill. For organizations that have already undergone a process orientation exercise, this set of business processes will already have been defined, and this step will

be completed quickly. For organizations where the business process concept has not been introduced, this is a very useful exercise that will produce highly valuable insight into which business processes are key activity areas of the business.

• Business process mapping and documentation, to the extent that the design team deems this step necessary, can be a useful exercise to draw additional, detailed pictures—both overall relationship maps and flowcharts—of some or all of the business processes. Since we have argued that one of the main focuses of the performance measurement system is the set of business processes, that is, attaching an instrument panel to each such process, this can be a worthwhile job at this stage. However, just like the previous step, this will probably be a superfluous task for organizations where business process orientation has already matured and business processes are well-known and part of everyday life.

The end result of this step of the performance measurement system design process should be a state of heightened awareness and insight into the overall business structure and business processes. This will constitute a foundation for developing a performance measurement system that actually measures what is important and contributes to the future success and development of the organization.

5.1 CLARIFICATION OF THE ORGANIZATION'S STRATEGY

Clarification of the organization's strategy should be a very brief task, the main purpose of which is simply to ensure that the design efforts followed during the entire performance measurement system design process build on a clearly defined, commonly agreed-upon, and thoroughly communicated strategy for the organization. All organizations should be able to articulate their strategy; if not, they are certainly not ready to develop and implement a state-of-the-art performance measurement system. An organization where this basic foundation is not in place has a much longer way to go to implement a performance measurement system, so we will assume that this is indeed in place and move on.

5.2 STAKEHOLDER ANALYSIS

As mentioned at the outset of this chapter, stakeholder analysis is not one generally agreed-upon analysis approach with certain steps to be performed. It is more of a commonsense exercise aimed at generating a higher awareness of the various stakeholders who have a vested interest in the organization and, at minimum, the needs, requirements, and expectations these stakeholders possess.

A company is surrounded by a number of stakeholders. The relationship between a stakeholder and the company is characterized by an exchange process. For example, customers receive products and pay money in return, suppliers receive money and provide services or products in return, and owners provide capital and receive dividends in return. Both the stakeholders and the company have a mutual interest in seeing that the organization achieves a high level of competitiveness, despite the fact that there will always be a discussion of distribution of benefits within this system. However, many of the stakeholders will have relationships with other companies, or at least the possibility of such multiple relationships exists. Thus, an organization's competitiveness is decided by its relative attractiveness toward the different stakeholders. Customers are in an exceptional position among the stakeholders, as they are the only source of payment or benefits to the other stakeholders, but the battle for the best ones applies to every type of stakeholder.

Competitiveness is decided by the relative attractiveness toward different stakeholders

This definition of competitiveness indicates that a company has to operate on several battlefields. Those companies that achieve the best products from suppliers, the best conditions from financial institutions, the best alliance partners, the best-qualified employees, and so on, have a competitive advantage. A consequence is that the performance measurement system must address several different target groups.

The only feasible way we have encountered for identifying these stakeholders is to conduct a good, old-fashioned brainstorming of the topic. If a small group of people from different areas of the organization gets together, they normally come up with the main stakeholders in an hour or two. If the performance measurement system design team has been composed so that representatives from different areas of the organization are indeed present, then this is a task well suited for the design team. Whoever undertakes this task of identifying the stakeholders, remember that there are some obvious and not so obvious stakeholders out there. The obvious ones are the customers, suppliers, perhaps owners, competitors, and employees. Some that are easy to overlook include partners, the media, government/authorities at various levels and of different types, the local community, and any number of pressure groups. Figure 5.1 illustrates how some of these stakeholders surround the organization and constitute important parts of the organization's environment.

The stakeholder examples in Figure 5.1 include alliance partners, and we would like to briefly draw your attention to this type of stakeholder before we proceed. Brandenburger and Nalebuff (1996) wrote a very good book on the concept of *co-opetition*, a term coined to illustrate that the

Co-opetition, the practice of both cooperating and competing

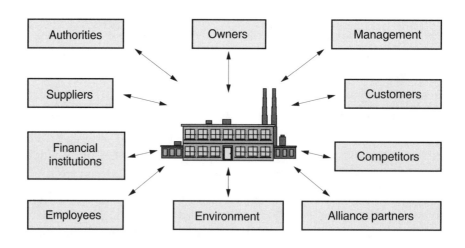

Figure 5.1   The stakeholder model.

only fitting metaphor to describe business is derived from war and the battlefield. They provided a number of excellent examples of situations where it pays off to cooperate in creating the pie and competing afterwards when deciding how to divide it. We will not delve deeply into these concepts, but one very important term defined in the book is a *complementor*. An actor in the business environment is a complementor of yours if customers value your product more when they also have the other player's product than when they have your product alone. An example is hot dogs and mustard—their vendors are complementors to each other and would benefit from some level of cooperation. When you find a cluster of car dealers along the same street, they cooperate to bring the car buyers to the area, but they compete to sell their cars to the buyers. This type of stakeholder is not in any special position over the others, but the concept is sufficiently novel to warrant extra attention, thus we encourage you to also think about complementors when analyzing your stakeholders. The so-called value net included in the Brandenburger and Nalebuff book can be a helpful view, as shown in Figure 5.2.

Ask the stakeholders what they want

All of these stakeholders, including the complementors, hold certain expectations of the organization. Identifying these expectations and translating them into more tangible quantities can probably be done by following different avenues. The organization probably already possesses a fairly high level of knowledge about some stakeholders' requirements, for example, owners or customers. For others, it might be difficult to tell what they really do, or perhaps do not, want. For pressure groups advocating equal opportunities, the media in general, or public authorities, the expectations are probably much less clearly understood and hidden agendas may even exist. No matter how you decide to approach this issue, the most straightforward way

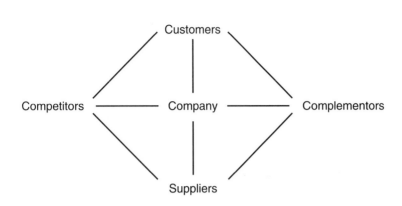

Figure 5.2 The value net of co-opetetition.

Source: From *Co-opetition* by Adam M. Brandenburger and Barry J. Nalebuff, copyright © 1996 by Adam M. Brandenburger and Barry J. Nalebuff. Used by permission of Doubleday, a division of Random House, Inc.

usually seems to be going to the source. First, this gives you the best first-hand access and insight into the true expectations of the organization's stakeholders. Second, most stakeholders react very positively and may even be flattered if they are approached this way, as it shows that you take them seriously and are concerned about their well-being and satisfaction with what you offer them. Such an approach will, of course, involve interaction with the stakeholders, but this is usually not a very time-consuming exercise and is certainly a learning experience for those who take part in it. We have never come across anyone who completed such an exercise without learning something truly surprising about the expectations of one or more stakeholders. You should also be aware that not all types of stakeholders need to be approached directly, for example, competitors or a long list of minor-position shareholders.

If you decide to engage the stakeholders in some kind of discussion about their expectations of the organization, there are again many ways of doing so. Your options include loose discussions, direct and more structured face-to-face interviews, phone interviews, or some type of survey. These all display strengths and weaknesses, and they are typically suited for different types of stakeholders. With owners, authorities, and other types of stakeholders, where relatively small numbers of individuals or organizations are involved, direct approaches such as discussions or interviews are good choices and often produce a rich information set. With employees, customers, or suppliers, where there are usually many more people involved, a survey is often a sound approach. This provides a larger data set, with better possibilities for various types of data analysis (which are beyond the scope of this book), although the data will not be as information-rich. If

Use direct contact with small groups of stakeholders and surveys for larger groups

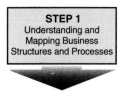

STEP 1
Understanding and
Mapping Business
Structures and Processes

***The Kano model
of expectations***

***Clearly expressed
requirements***

Basic requirements

supplemented by interviews with smaller groups of people, a deeper insight can also be gained from employees, customers, or suppliers.

If you actually try to map all of the probable and improbable expectations your stakeholders might divulge, you will undoubtedly discover that these are plentiful, not always coherent, and very wide-ranging. To bring some order to these expectations and be able to differentiate between the important and not so important ones, a very useful diagram called the Kano model is at your fingertips. As you can see from Figure 5.3, it is basically nothing more than an awareness-creating diagram showing that there are different types and levels of stakeholder requirements.

The straight diagonal line of the figure portrays the clearly expressed requirements of the stakeholder. Generally, these are the only demands the stakeholder will describe if being asked about her or his desires. If the stakeholder is a major shareholder of the organization, he could express requirements that the return on investment should be a minimum of 7.2 percent, that he be granted a seat on the board, and so on.

In addition, there also exists a set of requirements that are so basic that they are not even expressed, as indicated by the lower curve. For the

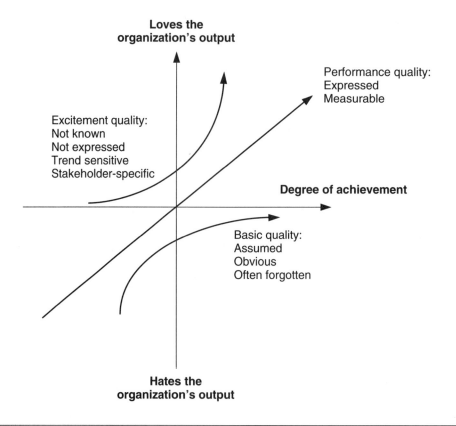

Figure 5.3   The Kano model and the three types of stakeholder requirements.

shareholder, these could be that the organization does not go broke and lose its capital, that it does not get involved in criminal or otherwise unethical activities that could harm the shareholders, that business is conducted according to general rules and customs, and so on.

Together, these two requirement sets constitute a complete set of demands imposed by the stakeholder on the organization. Their satisfaction depends on how well both sets of requirements have been satisfied. It will be of no help if the investment returns 10 percent if the shareholder is arrested for his involvement with the company due to criminal activities it has engaged in. In other words, satisfying expressed requirements cannot rectify shortcomings in the basic demands. On the other hand, satisfying every single one of the basic requirements will not lead to complete satisfaction unless the expressed requirements have also been fulfilled. This will, at best, eliminate dissatisfaction. The danger is that the stakeholder takes it for granted that the organization is aware of the basic requirements, while this might not be the case. Such silent assumptions are one of the main focuses when clarifying requirements in the stakeholder analysis.

If these two sets of requirements are defined and satisfied, the foundation for satisfaction should be firmly established. To further enhance satisfaction, and even create delight for the stakeholder, we can look to the third set of requirements. "Requirements" is not really the correct word, as these are conditions not expressed by the stakeholder, and often the stakeholder itself is not even aware of these needs. For the shareowner, this could include having the organization make all arrangements for transportation to general assemblies, free access to the organization's products or services, a special Web site for the shareholders that presents updated information of interest to them, and so on. If both the basic and expressed requirements have been satisfied, the fulfillment of such extra "requirements" can create true delight. These are often the little extras required to ensure loyalty and access to the best stakeholders of all kinds. You should note, though, that if such extra requirements are delivered one or more times, they are often added to the expressed or even basic requirements that must be fulfilled to avoid dissatisfaction.

To recap, the end outcome of the stakeholder analysis should be:

- A good understanding of who the organization's stakeholders are

- Insight into these stakeholders' expectations

- A classification of the expectations, preferably according to the three classes of requirements explained by the Kano model or some other type of ranking as to their importance

Excitement requirements

The outcome of a stakeholder analysis

STEP 1
Understanding and
Mapping Business
Structures and Processes

This constitutes a very good start to the web of silver threads that run from the stakeholders of the organization, through their expectations, and down to the business processes needed to fulfill them. The next step is therefore to identify and map these business processes.

5.3 BUSINESS PROCESS IDENTIFICATION

Depending on the familiarity of your organization with the concept of business processes and to what extent you have already moved toward process orientation and organization, this can be either a very difficult or a very simple task.

By now, many companies have realized the advantages of streamlining their activities along the value-adding business processes that run through their organizations. If you are among them, you probably have a very clear understanding of what your business processes are, what they look like, and how they work. If so, you can safely skip over or skim very quickly through this section.

Two routes to business process identification

If your organization has not begun any work to identify or create awareness around these logical chains of activities—business processes—then you have some work to do before proceeding. This can at times be rather difficult, as it is rarely obvious which processes are undertaken or contributed to by the various departments in a functionally organized enterprise. At least two routes to such an understanding can be taken. The most direct way is to simply generate a list of the business processes believed to be encompassed by the organization. Such a job will often be based on existing process descriptions or procedures written for ISO 9000 certification or similar purposes.

Types of business processes

Generating this can certainly be a challenging job, but there might be some help found in different attempts at classifying business processes into different groups of processes. Such efforts have been undertaken by a number of (often large) companies, for example Xerox and IBM. Other models have been designed to cover specific industries, for example, manufacturing, banking, IT, and air transportation. If you want to make use of such models, our advice is to seek out the one that seems to fit your type of organization best. Just to give you a feel for what groups of processes are typically defined, we have included an example developed for manufacturing enterprises, where the business processes are divided into the following three sets:

1. *Primary processes;* the central and value-creating processes of the enterprise. They run straight through the company, from activities on the customer side to receiving supplies from vendors.

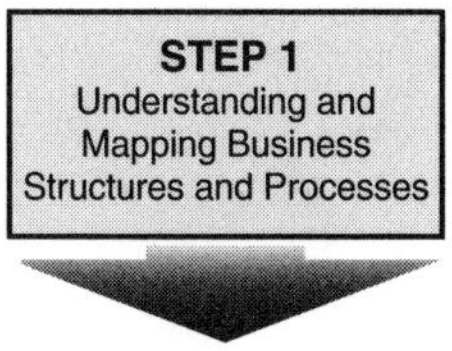

Primary processes	Secondary processes
Product development • Product research • Product engineering and design • Process engineering and design • Co-engineering	*Support* • Financial management • Human resource management • Information management • Maintenance • Internal control of health, environment, and safety
Obtaining customer commitment • Market development • Marketing and sales • Tendering	
Order fulfillment • Procurement and inbound logistics • Production planning and control • Manufacturing and assembly • Distribution and outbound logistics • Order processing	*Evolution* • Continuous business process improvement • Product research • Production technology research • Human resource development • Supplier Base development • Development of external relations • Strategic planning
Customer service • After-sales service • Product returns	

STEP 1
Understanding and Mapping Business Structures and Processes

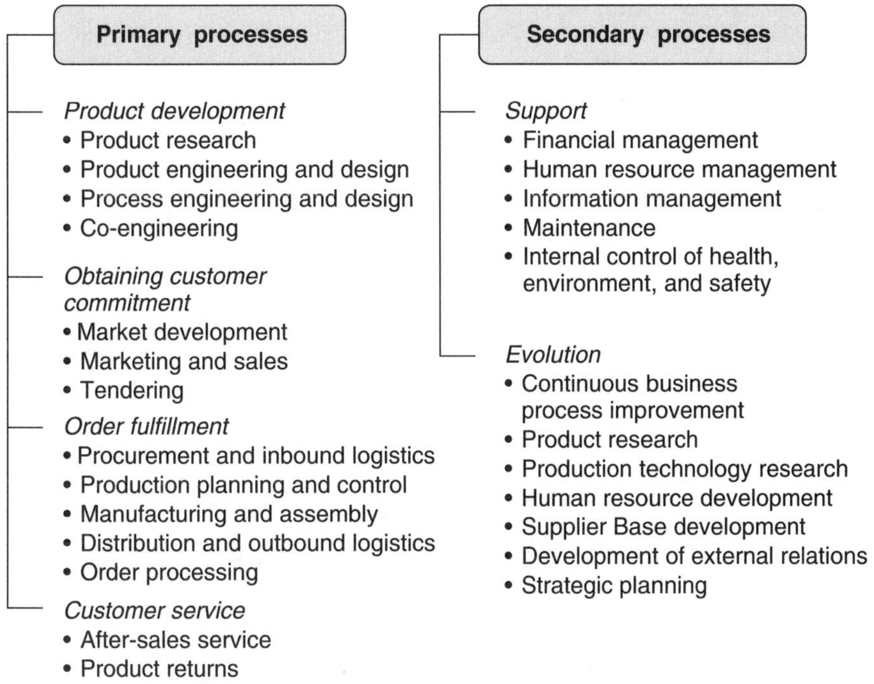

Figure 5.4   One possible division of business processes into groups.

2. *Support processes;* not direct value-creating processes, but rather activities needed to support the primary processes. This includes finance and personnel management.

3. *Developmental or evolution processes;* processes that are supposed to bring the organization and its primary and support processes to a higher level of performance. Examples are product research and supplier base development.

The corresponding framework of business processes is shown in Figure 5.4. Since this example is included as an illustration, we will not go into any details of these business processes. Other industries will display completely different processes, so this is an activity you must tailor to your own specific organization.

A more rewarding and systematic route to business process identification follows this pre-established chain of silver threads through the sequence of: (1) the strategy of the organization, which defines and is shaped by (2) stakeholders—organizations, institutions, or persons affected by or with a vested interest in the organization and its business processes—who hold (3) expectations, with regard to products or services delivered by the organization through (4) the business processes, that produce these products or services and support and enable their production.

Sample business process model

STEP 1
Understanding and
Mapping Business
Structures and Processes

By going through this set of elements and identifying them in sequence, it is much easier to point to the business processes performed by the organization that are necessary to fulfill the expectations of its stakeholders. By moving backward from the output to the stakeholders through primary and support processes and their input, several strings of business processes emerge. Even if this approach does not cover every conceivable process ever performed by the organization, this might actually be just as well. Processes not encountered when backtracking from the stakeholders' expectations are hardly crucial in providing satisfaction to them. Thus, if omitted, they will rarely be missed.

5.4 BUSINESS PROCESS MAPPING AND DOCUMENTATION

*Documenting
processes always
leads to improve-
ment ideas*

Just like the previous step of identifying your business processes, this step is superfluous if your organization is already working along business processes and has mapped and documented them. If not, it is still not a prerequisite that this step be performed to design your state-of-the-art performance measurement system, but the insight and knowledge gained from its execution is extremely valuable when putting together the instrument panel for each of these business processes. In addition, going through your business processes in a systematic manner and drawing flowcharts of them *always* leads to a wealth of ideas on how these processes can be improved, optimized, and harmonized with respect to each other. Taken to the fullest extent, this can be a very extensive job, so it might be wise to perform it in parallel with the performance measurement system design process. The possible complexity of the job also means that within the scope of this book we will have to limit the treatment of the topic to a minimum. There are, however, numerous good books on the market dealing exclusively with process mapping, for example, Dianne Galloway's *Mapping Work Processes* (1994).

One problem often faced when documenting business processes through flowcharts is that it is hard to know where to begin. It probably sounds like a straightforward job to draw a flowchart for a business process, but it can be difficult to figure out the starting point, the order of events, and, not in the least, the people involved in the process or with whom it interacts. We have found that this job is made much easier by taking a slightly less direct route, through a hierarchy of three different charts (where one of them can easily be skipped). These are shown in Figure 5.5, and serve the following purposes:

Process Overview

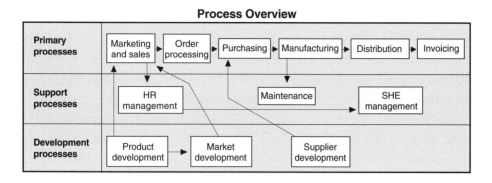

Relationship Map

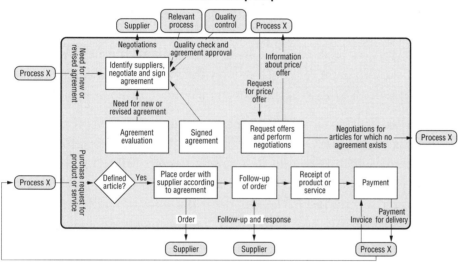

Flowchart

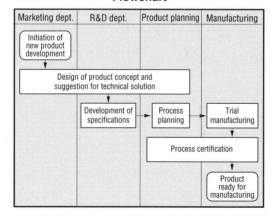

Figure 5.5   A hierarchy of process mapping charts.

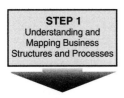

*A hierarchy of
business process
mapping charts:
1. Process overview
2. Relationship map
3. Flowchart*

• The process overview is intended to give a complete overview of the business processes performed in the organization. In Figure 5.5, there are a limited number of processes, thus making the chart quite readable. If you add every single one of your processes, chances are the chart will do more harm than good, so show some moderation when using the process overview chart. The point is to place the most important processes in a larger context and show how these are related. However, this is the chart that can be left out, especially if you feel this aspect is quite clear and you want to get going with documenting the individual business processes.

• The relationship map goes directly into one business process and takes a less detailed look at it than a flowchart. This chart is meant to show the main tasks of the process and, in particular, how it interacts with other processes, external actors, or other elements in its surroundings. It usually provides an excellent starting point for construction of the actual flowchart, since it has placed the process in its environment and identified its main steps.

• The flowchart is the ordinary diagram type used by everyone mapping their business processes. It can take on a few different styles, for example, by indicating which person or department is responsible for carrying out different steps, adding time or cost accumulation data, or decomposing processes on several levels. The fundamental rules are still the same, and the main purpose is to give a graphical view of the steps in the process.

The charts in Figure 5.5 are extremely useful for gaining further insight into business processes to define their best possible performance measurement instrument panel. The process overview chart helps the performance measurement system design team identify performance indicators that span several individual business processes to encourage an overall best possible performance, thus avoiding any propensity for suboptimization within business processes. The relationship map is ideal for identifying the transactions that occur between the business process and its surroundings. For the most important of these transactions, performance indicators should be defined that help the people executing the process to keep track of and improve stakeholder satisfaction for the individual process. Finally, the flowchart can be used directly to define performance indicators that measure the speed, quality, cost, environmental impact, and so on, of the process and its steps.

The next step of the performance measurement system design process is the development of business performance priorities. But before continuing, it might be pertinent to put your mind at ease regarding the number of performance indicators you will eventually end up with in your state-of-the-art performance measurement system. From what you have read so far, you are probably thinking that with all the indicators proposed—for the organization at a higher level, for strings of business processes, for transactions between business processes, and numerous indicators within each process—there will be loads of indicators in this performance measurement system! We hope we can convince you that what we have been talking about so far are mainly *possibilities* for measurement, not *everything* that you should measure. Later on in the design process, we will address the issue of how many indicators are feasible to monitor simultaneously, the human mind's limitations with regard to this aspect, and some rules of thumb for choosing performance indicators.

STEP 1
Understanding and Mapping Business Structures and Processes

Don't kill the organization with hundreds of performance indicators

5.5 BUSINESS STRUCTURE AND PROCESS UNDERSTANDING AND MAPPING IN PBI, I³M

As you may recall from the introduction of this case study, PBI, I³M started a larger project termed PBI, I³M Business Excellence. This project was divided into two subprojects—process orientation and performance measurement system design—with a steering committee overseeing the entire project. "Our" subproject, the performance measurement system design, was established with a project manager chosen from a small group of people running the company's data warehouse, who was given free reign to pick the design team members. Four were appointed: the quality manager, the vice president, a very talented sales representative, and an operator from complaints handling.

The team started the project by running through the substeps of this initial phase in the design process, and first of all looked at the defined strategy for PBI, I³M. This was readily available, as quite a lot of work had been put into strategy formulation in conjunction with the establishment of PBI, I³M as an independent company. Briefly recited, the main strategic objectives were to:

1. Be perceived as a reliable and cost-efficient supplier of IT infrastructure management services for all internal clients within the People's Bank & Insurance group.

2. Enable improved and innovative services on the part of these internal clients through constant introduction of new technology and new solutions.

3. Increase the customer portfolio by capturing external clients representing at least 25 percent of revenues.

The strategy also contained the obligatory position that the company should be profitable, generate earnings for its owners (the People's Bank &

Insurance holding company), provide an attractive work place for its employees, and so on. All in all, this gave the team quite a clear direction for its further work, with emphasis on developing a performance measurement system geared toward customer satisfaction.

To gain an even better perspective of the organization's environment, a coarse stakeholder model (as shown in Figure 5.6) was designed by means of a brainstorming session.

Coming from a "protected" position as an internal department within the PBI group, the stakeholder picture was not very complex. Understanding their expectations and requirements was not as easy, though. The design team decided on an interview approach, with each team member conducting talks with selected stakeholder representatives. Some expectations surfaced immediately, but for a couple of the stakeholders, the team had to go through several rounds of discussions before truly understanding their demands. The main expectations identified of PBI, I3M were as follows:

- PBI, I3M Holding Company:

    - Generate an annual profit margin of 6 percent.

    - Keep costs for the internal PBI customers as low as possible.

    - Be a responsive partner for the PBI customers in the development of new services for external banking and insurance customers.

- PBI internal customers:

    - Maintain an average system up-time of 97 percent for all IT subsystems.

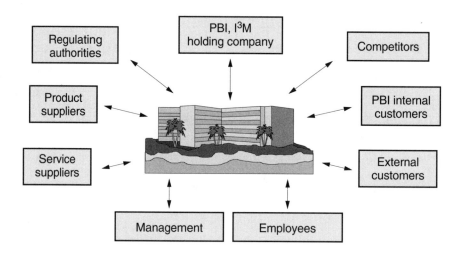

Figure 5.6   PBI, I³M stakeholder model.

- Set limits for complaint handling times for different categories of problems.

- Reduce annual costs by 3 percent for all major existing services.

- Be an active initiator of and participant in efforts to develop new services for their customers.

STEP 1
Understanding and
Mapping Business
Structures and Processes

- External customers: These requirements turned out to be almost identical to those of the internal customers, but, surprisingly enough, often with looser limits for aspects like system up-time, problem resolution times, and so on.

- Product and service suppliers: Although the suppliers were not in the same position as the customers or owner when it came to imposing demands on PBI, I³M, they did have their expectations, mainly regarding the volume of future business and timely payment for products delivered or services rendered.

- Management and employees: These two groups were strikingly similar in their expectations, which mainly covered issues such as pay levels, reasonable working hours, quality of work life, benefits, and other expected elements. Additionally, surprising issues were also uncovered, for example, that many employees expected remuneration and share option packages in line with other IT companies, continued training and education, and support for home offices.

- Regulating authorities: This was a rather complex stakeholder to relate to, since it consisted of many different entities, including administrations overseeing storage of personal and confidential information, banking security issues, taxes, workers' welfare, and so on. Once these had been identified, they were nevertheless easier to relate to in terms of demands, as most of them were clearly articulated by laws and regulations.

- Competitors: PBI, I³M has no internal competitors, but there are plenty of other companies specializing in taking over the responsibility for IT infrastructure when firms decide to outsource these services. In terms of being stakeholders for PBI, I³M, competitors naturally hope to gain entrance into the PBI group as well as resist attempts from PBI, I³M to obtain contracts with external customers. None of the competitors identified held any expectations of cooperation, partnership, or coordinated market sharing.

STEP 1
Understanding and
Mapping Business
Structures and Processes

Alongside the performance measurement system design subproject, the team working on the process orientation part of the business excellence project progressed with their work. Partly based on input from the stakeholder analysis and partly by mapping current activities, the process overview chart shown in Figure 5.7 emerged. This is a highly complex diagram, but we have included it to illustrate PBI, I³M's approach to this task, which is quite different from the example shown in Figure 5.5. This also goes to show that there are many different ways of drawing such process models, as there is no generally accepted standard in use worldwide. Perhaps this is not even a negative feature; we always feel that the most important aspect of such modeling is that the users—your organization—feel comfortable with the "standard" in use, not that you adhere strictly to a global ISO standard or its equivalent.

The process orientation team proceeded to construct both relationship maps and detailed flowcharts for all of these processes; in most cases there were several flowcharts for each process. We have decided not to include one of these here, since it will not add to your understanding of this case. Anyway, the team completed this step of the design process with a good feeling of accomplishment and charged on—the story continues at the end of the next chapter.

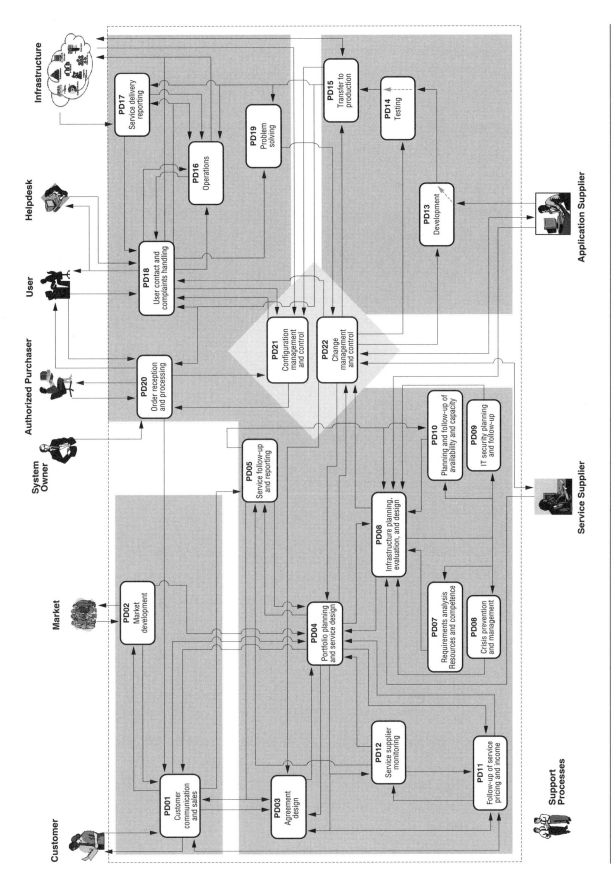

Figure 5.7 Process overview chart displaying 22 processes (PDs).

Chapter 6

Step 2: Developing Business Performance Priorities

STEP 1
Understanding and Mapping Business Structures and Processes

STEP 2
Developing Business Performance Priorities

STEP 3
Understanding the Current Performance Measurement System

STEP 4
Developing Performance Indicators

STEP 5
Deciding How to Collect the Required Data

STEP 6
Designing Reporting and Performance Data Presentation Formats

STEP 7
Testing and Adjusting the Performance Measurement System

STEP 8
Implementing the Performance Measurement System

In the previous step of the performance measurement system design process, we showed you how to identify a string of logically connected elements from the organization's strategy through its stakeholders down to its business processes. Along the way, we addressed the requirements and expectations of the stakeholders, but at a rather qualitative level and for the main purpose of gaining and refreshing the insight and awareness of the organization, its surroundings, and its business processes. In this step, the main objective is to go into more detail of performance requirements and priorities posed by both the organization's strategy and the stakeholders. We will also demonstrate one specific tool that can be applied during this exercise—quality function deployment adapted to performance planning.

6.1 QUANTIFYING THE STAKEHOLDERS' PERFORMANCE REQUIREMENTS

As should be apparent from the stakeholder model depicted in Figure 5.1, the very diverse set of stakeholders any organization must relate to will have very different needs and expectations of that organization. While it would be miraculously beneficial if all of these needs and expectations were in harmony with each other, it is not very likely to happen. Different stakeholders feel strongly about different aspects of the organization and its activities and outputs—there are bound to be some conflicting interests. Further, the various stakeholders will most definitely place different priorities within their sets of requirements (as demonstrated in the Kano model,

see Figure 5.3). Thus, there is a need for clarifying this "mess" by performing a more systematic analysis, whose main objective is a prioritization of the different requirements.

The way we have outlined this exercise, there are three issues to address, as illustrated in Figure 6.1. The natural way to run through this sequence of steps is to let the performance measurement system design team take the lead and either perform them within the team or let groups throughout the organization perform individual rankings and then merge them afterwards. The former is obviously quicker, but the latter will normally both tap better into the knowledge of the entire work force and, not in the least, contribute to the ownership of the resulting performance measurement system throughout the organization. The three issues are:

*Three issues
to address*

1. Recall the set of stakeholders identified previously, and now rank them in terms of relative importance to the organization. The ranking is done by attaching values from 1 to 10, with 1 being of little importance and 10 of the utmost importance to the organization.

2. Think of the needs and expectations that, ideally, should also have been identified, and now translate these into more specific performance requirements for the organization.

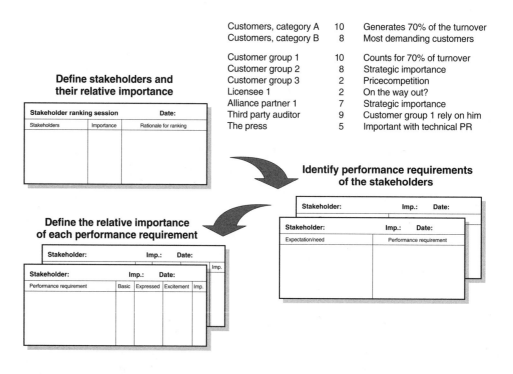

Figure 6.1   A sequence of stakeholder and performance requirement prioritizations.

STEP 2
Developing Business
Performance Priorities

3. For each of these performance requirements, make an assessment of which set of expectations they belong to according to the Kano model (basic, expressed, or able to excite) and their relative importance. This latter importance ranking can be done either by using the same scale as for the stakeholder ranking (1 to 10) or by taking the importance ranking of the stakeholder from which the requirement originates and multiplying the stakeholder importance factor with the requirement importance factor, producing a compound value reflecting both aspects.

The forms shown in Figure 6.1 are aids you can employ when running through this prioritization exercise, and their use will be illustrated in the continuation of the PBI, I³M example at the end of this chapter.

Examples of completed forms are shown in the case at the end of the chapter

When attaching an importance ranking to the different stakeholders, you should keep in mind that getting this ranking right could help you exploit the resources of the organization more effectively. Identifying that a stakeholder has a vested interest in your organization is not the same as saying you should put massive resources into satisfying that stakeholder's expectations. Figure 6.2 is a reminder of the necessity to maximize the cost/benefit ratio of investments in the satisfaction of various stakeholders. For some, it might not be worth the effort to follow a maximum satisfaction strategy, whereas for others this can be crucial.

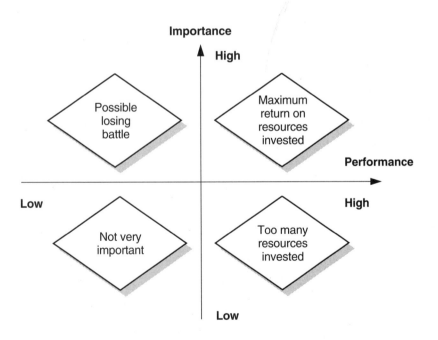

Figure 6.2 Stakeholder importance and suitable resource investments for their satisfaction.

Issues that decide different stakeholders' importance to your organization

Typical issues that affect the importance of the different stakeholders are:

- Financial impact the stakeholder can have on the organization

- The availability of alternative stakeholders

- The general attractiveness of the stakeholder

- The competitive position of the stakeholder

- Investments made in the relationship with the stakeholder

- Strategic importance of the stakeholder

You have now identified the stakeholders' general expectations of and the needs to be satisfied by the organization. By performing this exercise, you will easily see that this is only halfway to understanding which requirements are needed for your organization. Say that the owners of the organization have been identified as an important group of stakeholders, and one of their expectations is that their connection with the organization does not result in any embarrassment due to dubious behavior by the organization. How does this translate into performance requirements for the organization? It doesn't directly, but indirectly this might impose the requirement that the organization should implement a business ethics program, take on some form of social responsibility, be more proactive toward quality of work life for its employees, and so on. In other situations, the relationship between stakeholder needs and performance requirements of the organization can be much more direct, but often they are not. In any case, the task of specifically trying to perform this translation is often worthwhile.

Finally, by ranking the importance of these performance requirements, you will have arrived at the essence of performance for your organization. By assessing the importance of each requirement, a rating of performance priorities from the stakeholder's point of view is obtained. This importance rating is one of the key inputs into the rest of the performance measurement system design process, in terms of achieving the desired alignment from stakeholders down to the performance indicators used throughout the organization.

6.2 STRATEGIC PERFORMANCE REQUIREMENTS

We have already explained how the strategy of the organization, in addition to the stakeholders' expectations, constitutes the other main element that should define and be reflected in the design of your state-of-the-art performance measurement system. As with the stakeholder expectations, the translation from the strategy into more specific requirements is not always entirely straightforward, so some type of translation and prioritization, similar to what was done for the stakeholder-induced requirements, must be performed. This basically involves converting strategic plans and decisions, with different timelines and at different levels of specificity, into more concrete performance requirements that the performance measurement system should then be able to monitor.

Both the timeline and the level of detail of the strategic plan elements determine to what extent they can be translated into requirements. If your vision is to develop communication technology for a better-connected society, you might have a hard time converting this vision into specific performance requirements that you can actually measure. If a lower-level element of the same strategic direction is to achieve 50 percent broadband coverage in private homes within three years, you probably will have no problems with translation into requirements for technology development, "productification" of the technology, installation capacity development, reasonable pricing, and so on.

The really "juicy" part of this approach lies in the often numerous conflicting requirements implied by different parts of the strategy. Usually any strategic plan is composed of decisions, objectives, defined directions, and so on, for different areas of the organization, market segments, or some other kind of division. While these might seem to be aligned with each other, many conflicts are discovered through their translation into specific requirements for the organization. Some of these are less serious and can be solved through prioritization among various strategic plan elements, while others must be resolved by adjusting the plans. No matter how this is handled, the exercise of converting the strategy into performance requirements is very useful, both in terms of identifying such conflicts and prioritizing among different elements of the strategy.

Just a small note before we move on: the development of strategic performance requirements should, to a much larger extent, be integrated into the strategic planning process, perhaps as some kind of feasibility study of different strategies, so that such conflicts can be eliminated earlier. Conflicts often arise between strategies generated from the bottom-up by different departments or business units within an enterprise. A striking example of this was found in a manufacturer of large diesel engines. The production department was concerned about the increasing number of sold engines that demanded some form of engineering or customer tailoring before they were released into production. This was very costly, as the company had no efficient system for handling this. Due to a change in the competitive environment, shorter delivery times and improved delivery rates were demanded by customers. Because of often-needed engineering and customer tailoring, valuable time was lost in the delivery process. The

Developing strategic performance requirements usually reveals conflicting priorities

STEP 2
Developing Business
Performance Priorities

Example of a completed form is shown in the case at the end of the chapter

manufacturing department hypothesized that the trouble was caused by a poor sales approach where customers were allowed to ask for specific alterations and the sales people were too weak to deny their requests. However, by coincidence, the engineering department discovered that offering more customer-tailored solutions was part of the marketing strategy.

In line with the simplified forms depicted in Figure 6.1, we have developed an easy-to-use small form that the performance measurement system design team might use when translating strategy into performance requirements. The form is shown in Figure 6.3, and our recommendation for accomplishing this step of the process is the same as for the stakeholder-related performance requirements. It is quicker if the design team does it; if more people are involved, it takes longer but better reflects the collective wisdom of the organization and consequently contributes to ownership of the design process.

Having identified performance requirements induced by the stakeholders' expectations and the organization's strategy, the final task in this step of the design process is to integrate these different requirements and prioritize them.

6.3 INTEGRATING THE DIFFERENT PERFORMANCE REQUIREMENTS

You might say that this is a task that goes way beyond designing a performance measurement system, and to some extent we would agree with that. However, we hope you will appreciate that designing and implementing a state-of-the-art performance measurement system, even if this system will be dynamic and change with altering business conditions, is a very effective way of enforcing the strategic direction of the organization. If you put much effort into designing a performance measurement system based on a strategic understanding that is poorly developed and harmonized, you risk either ending up with a performance measurement system that is not very useful or having this less-than-ideal strategic direction effectively enforced

Strategy:	Imp.:	Date:
Performance requirement		Importance

Figure 6.3 Converting strategy into performance requirements.

by the measurement system. Either way, the outcome is negative, so make sure that these steps toward a sound strategic direction are taken to avoid either of these outcomes—and it forces the organization to do something that should have been completed already anyway.

What we are really looking for is to develop a common understanding of the company priorities that are being expressed in this often-mentioned strategic direction. Since there are bound to be many different views of the strategic and organizational direction, we need an approach that can integrate all of the resulting performance requirements and provide some insight into how they conflict, support each other, or are unrelated.

Luckily, such an approach has already been developed, albeit for a slightly different purpose. Many of you are probably familiar with the concept of quality function deployment (QFD). QFD was initially developed to represent a customer-oriented approach to product development. For this usage, it is a methodology for structuring customer needs, expectations, and requirements and translating them into detailed product and process specifications. The principles can, however, also be used for a number of other problems, including performance requirement prioritization through the application of the structured approach represented by QFD.

The QFD approach is built around populating a possibly complex diagram often referred to as the "house of quality," at the heart of which is a so-called relational matrix. This relational matrix is illustrated in Figure 6.4.

What constitutes the goals of the analysis, which in the case of the original application of QFD—product development—are customer requirements and expectations. In our case of performance requirement prioritization, *what* is the stakeholder and strategy-related performance requirements. *How* expresses the means to reach these goals: in the case of product development, technical product concepts; in our case, business processes or other activities of the organization. In the relational matrix

STEP 2
Developing Business
Performance Priorities

QFD was originally developed for product development

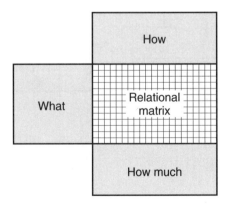

Figure 6.4   The basic structure of the QFD diagram.

field, a weight factor for each element of *what* is multiplied with a grade indicating how well each element of *how* contributes to satisfying the *what* requirements. Thus, an indicator for the performance of each *how* element is generated, which is placed in the field *how much*. This way, the various business processes or other aspects of the organization can be ranked based on their contribution to the collective set of performance requirements facing the organization. The nice feature of the QFD methodology is that this ensures that the complete set of requirements are included in the prioritization of which activities will be important and how they will be measured in the performance measurement system. In fact, since product development involves several stages of gradual progress toward a complete product, each phase of the product development process is linked together as a chain of relational matrices, as shown in Figure 6.5, to ensure that the voice of the customer is transmitted throughout the entire process. The same principle can be applied in the type of strategy-translated-to-business-process-planning that we are dealing with here.

The house of quality

During the QFD process, additional information can be added to create a full chart known as the house of quality (due to its shape), as depicted in Figure 6.6.

The QFD process enters data into each room of the house of quality. *What*, as already explained, represents the performance requirements. To each *what* element, a weight factor is attached expressing the element's importance, which renders it possible to emphasize some requirements more strongly than others. *Why* represents "challenges" facing the organization, which are normally offers made by other organizations toward your stakeholders. The most obvious offers are, of course, competitors targeting your customers, but other examples include competitive companies trying

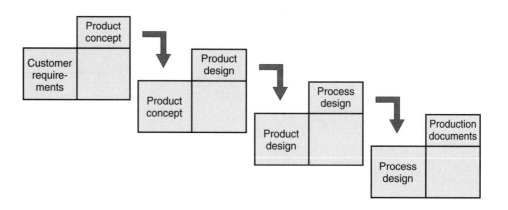

Figure 6.5 A chain of QFD charts.

STEP 2
Developing Business
Performance Priorities

to attract your employees, ventures seeking investors, and so on. These challenges can be expressed by benchmarking the offers and performance of different "competitors."

After determining how the performance requirements can be fulfilled— *how*—the relational matrix linking *what* and *how* is completed. To make the matrix as clear as possible, it is usually preferable to use as few types of relations as possible. A set of commonly used symbols is shown in Figure 6.7. In the same manner, the roof of the house of quality forms a relational matrix to be used for investigating whether there are any relationships between the different elements of *how*. In this matrix, it is possible to indicate both positive and negative relations, that is, factors that work together or that create trade-offs or conflicts. Some common symbols for this matrix are indicated in Figure 6.8.

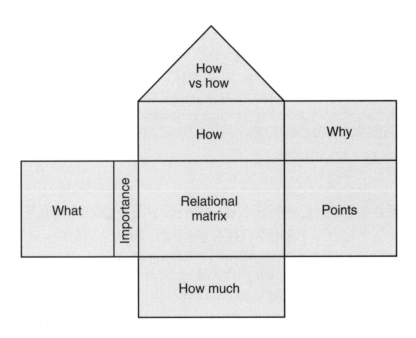

Figure 6.6 The house of quality.

Relation	Symbol	Weight
Weak	△	1
Medium	○	3
Strong	◉	9

Figure 6.7 Symbols for the relational matrix.

Relationship	Symbol
Strong positive	◉
Weak positive	○
Weak negative	✕
Strong negative	✖

Figure 6.8   Symbols for the roof matrix.

For each *how*, the identified relationship's weight factor to the individual elements of *what* is multiplied with the corresponding factor for each requirement element's importance. All products are summarized and placed in the lower field of the chart, *how much*. Business processes or activities of *how* with a high score in this field should be prioritized and measured, since they represent an ability to satisfy the collective set of performance requirements. In the end, these are the results that should be brought forward from this performance prioritization effort and into the ensuing steps of the performance measurement system design process. The QFD approach may seem confusing—which it certainly can be after such a general introduction—but we hope that the continuation of the PBI, I³M case will clarify its specific use.

6.4 DEVELOPING BUSINESS PERFORMANCE PRIORITIES IN PBI, I³M

In the previous chapter, we left PBI, I³M at the point where the performance measurement system design team had identified and documented the most important business processes. To further understand and prioritize the more specific performance requirements facing PBI, I³M, the team went on to specify in more detail what the various stakeholders' expectations meant to the organization.

To create as much knowledge about this part of the PBI, I³M Business Excellence project as possible, 10 teams scattered throughout the organization were asked to go through the series of rankings from stakeholders down to the importance of each specific performance requirement. This was accomplished using the forms shown in Figure 6.1, and we will present an example of each of these here, both to show you how they can be used and to illustrate the thinking done in PBI, I³M. This exercise resulted in a total of approximately 200 such forms from the 10 teams, but we will only show the examples found in Figure 6.9.

STEP 2
Developing Business
Performance Priorities

Stakeholder ranking session   **Date: 05.13**

Stakeholders	Importance	Rationale for ranking
PBI, I³M holding company	5	Stable, not very active owner
PBI internal customers	10	Accounts for > 90% of the turnover
External customers	8	Stepping stones to other customers
Product/service suppliers	3	Not very critical
Management/employees	9	Important, scarce resource
Regulating authorities	3	Must be abided by, no positive effects
Competitors	5	Important for external customers

Stakeholder: Employees   **Imp.: 9   Date: 05.19**

Expectation/need	Performance requirement
Stable and attractive jobs	Financial solidity
Competitive pay level	Offer sufficient wages
Attractive work conditions	Provide good SHE conditions
Reasonable working hours	Establish practical shift schedules
Share options	Difficult to offer!
Continued training and education	Continuous competence mapping and planning
Home office offer	Implement a home office system

Stakeholder: Employees   **Imp.: 9   Date: 05.19**

Performance requirement	Basic	Expressed	Excitement	Imp.
Financial solidity	*			5
Offer sufficient wages		*		10
Provide good SHE conditions	*			7
Establish practical shift schedules		*		7
Continuous competence mapping and planning			*	5
Implement a home office system			*	3

Figure 6.9   Examples of assessments made of stakeholders, performance requirements, and their importance.

Next, a similar exercise was undertaken to translate the strategy into performance requirements, as illustrated in the example form in Figure 6.10.

Following these two introductory performance requirements identification steps, the real job at this stage involved using the QFD diagram to prioritize the performance requirements. The diagram itself (in a somewhat simplified version) is shown in Figure 6.11, and we will take you through each of the areas of this house of quality.

Again, this chart is rather simplified, so bear with us if there were considerations made earlier in the process that are not really reflected here—the main point is to illustrate how the QFD approach can be effectively employed for this prioritization purpose.

First, the performance requirements field was completed by inserting the performance requirements identified earlier through the stakeholder

Strategy: Provide attractive places of work	Imp.: 9 Date: 05.31
Performance requirement	Importance
Maintain practical and inviting buildings	6
Encourage a friendly and positive atmosphere	8
Keep pay levels and benefits at competitive levels	8
Implement routines to capture employee suggestions for improvements	5
Continuously develop the competence of the employees	10

Figure 6.10   An example of a conversion of strategy into performance requirements.

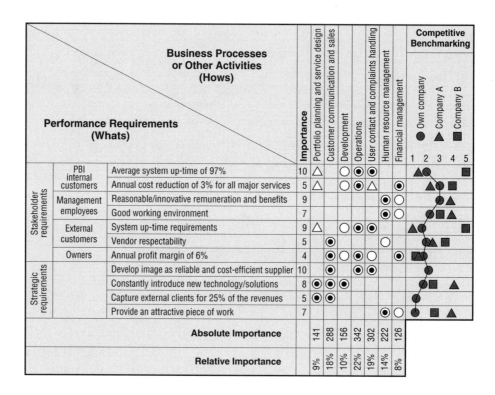

Figure 6.11   Simplified QFD chart for the integration of stakeholder and strategic performance requirements.

analysis and strategy clarification (only a selection has been included in the example). Each requirement was assigned an importance rating, which should, of course, correspond with the ratings designated earlier in the process (see Figure 6.9). For each requirement, a limited competitive benchmarking was completed by the performance measurement system design team based on their collective insight into two competitors in the external market.

Next, the identified business processes were inserted into the *how* field, which was the means to satisfy the requirements (again only a selection). Using their best judgment, impact symbols were assigned to each of the requirement/business process combinations of the relationship matrix (empty fields indicate no impact). Using the corresponding numerical impact factor for each of the impact symbols (see Figure 6.7), the products of the importance ratings and impacts were generated and summed up for each business process. Just to make sure this is clear, let us explain this in more detail for one of the business processes.

For user contact and complaints handling, the calculation is as follows:

- There is an impact factor of 9 for average system up-time, which carries an importance rating of 10; this gives a product value of 90.

- An impact factor of 3, or medium impact, for annual cost reduction, multiplied by the importance rating of 5, gives a value of 15.

- An impact factor of 9 for external customers' system up-time requirements with the importance of 9, gives a total of 81.

- A factor of 1, or a low impact assessment, for annual profit margin, with an importance rating of 4, gives a product value of 4.

- An impact factor of 9 for image development, with an importance weight of 10, gives a value of 90.

- The total sum expressing how much this business process is able to impact the collective set of performance requirements is 302, as can be seen in the *how much* field.

The *how much* field has been split into two here, with the first carrying the total impact value. In the case of user contact and complaints handling, the value is 302. The problem with this value is that it did not tell the team very much. Therefore, relative importance figures were calculated in the last field of the diagram, giving an impact rating of 19 percent.

In this very simple example, the variation between the different *how* elements was not extensive. In a complete sample, this variation will normally be much larger, thus giving a clearer picture of what is important to measure. In the PBI, I³M case, the complete chart did provide valuable insight. The resulting relative importance figures for the entire set of business processes made it much easier for the team to prioritize which business processes could be taken lightly, and in the development of which

performance indicators they should invest their resources. The results were also used later on when deciding which performance data to include in reports being sent upward through the organizational hierarchy.

The next chapter will take you through the step of assessing your current performance measurement system and to what extent parts of it are suitable for inclusion in your new, state-of-the-art system.

Chapter 7

Step 3: Understanding the Current Performance Measurement System

STEP 1
Understanding and Mapping Business Structures and Processes

STEP 2
Developing Business Performance Priorities

STEP 3
Understanding the Current Performance Measurement System

STEP 4
Developing Performance Indicators

STEP 5
Deciding How to Collect the Required Data

STEP 6
Designing Reporting and Performance Data Presentation Formats

STEP 7
Testing and Adjusting the Performance Measurement System

STEP 8
Implementing the Performance Measurement System

Having completed the introductory and awareness-stimulating first two steps, you must decide at this point how much you will build upon any pre-existing performance measurement system. Assuming that your organization has some sort of formal or informal measurement system in place, we will now discuss how to understand this system. In our experience, the following steps are useful for determining whether or not to reuse parts of the current performance measurement system:

1. Obtain a rough overview of the current performance measurement system, that is, what it contains in terms of performance indicators, data collection and storage functionality, presentation tools, and so on.

2. Analyze to what degree the existing system infrastructure or its elements may be incorporated into the new system.

3. Review the existing performance indicators in order to analyze which ones may be used in the new system.

This brief chapter will take you through each of these steps.

7.1 OBTAIN AN OVERVIEW OF THE CURRENT PERFORMANCE MEASUREMENT SYSTEM

The first aspect has been previously unmentioned. We feel that a good starting point is to understand the degree of ownership felt for the existing

*Four combinations
of attitudes toward
the existing system*

performance measurement system. Management and other employees harbor four basic combinations of attitudes toward the system:

1. The employees have strong positive feelings for the existing system, but management does not share these feelings. This is an indication that you should be careful in making any changes to the system or planning the implementation of a completely new one. It might, however, also be an argument for scrapping the existing system altogether and starting from scratch. This will avoid having the employees continue to use the old system informally and either disregard or sabotage the new one.

2. Management has strong positive feelings for the existing system while the employees do not share this opinion. This is also an argument for scrapping the old system. The employees will more likely give a completely new system a chance.

3. Both management and employees have high regards for the existing system. This might be used as an argument for using parts of the old system. However, you should be careful about this approach to avoid having the old parts dominate the system, in which case it will hardly be any better than the one you have.

4. Neither management nor the employees like the old system. We would suggest that you throw out the entire system and start all over.

*Understanding
an informal
existing system*

When striving to obtain this rough overview of the current system, the approach used will differ depending on whether the current system is formal or informal. If you don't have a formal performance measurement system, but you have an informal one for collecting and reporting data, then obtaining an overview of the current system is a more cumbersome process. In this case, the design team probably will have to analyze each department or business process in order to understand what is being measured and how. Such a set of analyses should be compiled into an overall image of which processes or areas are indeed measured today and which are not. For those processes or areas covered by measurements, the aspects of measurement frequency, how the measurements are collected, by whom, and so on, need to be understood (these aspects are treated in more detail in chapter 9). In addition, the team should seek to understand how these measures are used and their reporting frequency—by whom and to whom.

*Mapping an existing
formal system*

If the current system is formal—one that has been deliberately designed and implemented as opposed to just emerging and being put to use—then it can be studied by reviewing the system itself and any documentation provided. If the system is applied daily, then users of the system can be interviewed to gain a deeper understanding of how the system operates. The system infrastructure should be roughly mapped at an aggregated level by employing an adapted version of the methodology described earlier in this book on business process mapping and documentation (see chapter 5).

Whether the existing system is formal or informal, the outcome of this step should merely be a coarse overview of the system infrastructure, that is, computerized modules, data collection routines, performance reports, and performance measures—the detailed, defined indicators. This overall mapping should not be accompanied by an assessment of the quality of these elements, as this has a tendency for biasing the produced documentation. Leave that evaluation to later steps.

STEP 3
Understanding the Current Performance Measurement System

The outcome of the mapping task

7.2 ANALYZE WHETHER PARTS OF THE EXISTING SYSTEM INFRASTRUCTURE CAN BE REUSED

The next step involves analyzing whether parts of the existing performance measurement system infrastructure can be reused. What criteria can be applied to decide this often hard-to-answer question? As is the case with several questions raised in this book, there is no generally agreed-upon set of criteria. However, we will try to provide you with a few hints. First, look at the routines and techniques for collecting data and how the collected performance data are analyzed, aggregated, and reported. In both instances, look into whether the system seems to work properly and without obvious sources of error or malfunction, its responsiveness to requests for performance data, its flexibility for further adaptation, and the time and cost required to run and maintain it. Further, the capability for granting all future users access to the performance measurement data is an essential aspect, and you should not ignore your general gut feeling regarding whether the system infrastructure has what it takes to constitute the core of your state-of-the-art system.

Advice for evaluating the existing system infrastructure

This last piece of advice exemplifies why it is difficult to provide any clear-cut criteria for deciding "yes, the old system is OK" or "no, let's get rid of it." Either assessment is very subjective—10 different people can end up with 10 different views on which parts can be reused and which must be scrapped. It is often a matter of personal preference, which can vary dramatically throughout the organization and depends upon the quality of the specific parts of the system that the individual user has been exposed to.

People's views of the existing system are very subjective

STEP 3
Understanding the
Current Performance
Measurement System

Therefore, it is generally a sound approach to talk to quite a few people within the organization, and then, in the end, follow your own instinct.

You should also try to look ahead when deciding the fate of the old system. As you will see in chapter 9, one major design choice is whether to go for a manual, paper-based system or a computer-based one. If the existing system consists of paper reports—albeit good ones—but you are ready for a modern, Web-based system, then the decision will be easier to make.

7.3 REVIEW THE EXISTING PERFORMANCE INDICATORS

*Three categories
for classifying the
old performance
indicators*

Whether or not you decide to reuse parts of the old system's infrastructure, its performance indicators can often be of good quality and it is wise to maintain them. Thus, the third and final step in this phase is to review the existing performance indicators and try to classify them as belonging in the following categories:

- Performance indicators that should be used in the new system

- Performance indicators that might be used in the new system

- Performance indicators that should not be used in the new system

The indicators in the first category support the performance priorities of the organization or its business processes, or are likely to foster a sound development of what is needed to fulfill these priorities. To map which indicators fit into this category, revisit and list the performance priorities clarified in chapter 5 along with feasible candidates for this category. Then try to determine whether a relationship exists between the priorities and each indicator.

The indicators in the second category are those that did not quite fit into the first category, but still were not too far off the mark. These might be indicators that are not quite in alignment with the business priorities, but still support them in a limited manner. The performance indicators from the "maybe" category might be used as they are or in a revised version in the new performance measurement system.

The third and last category contains the indicators you should not use in the new system. Examples include indicators that are irrelevant to the performance priorities; that are both counterproductive and likely to counteract the desired effects, and hidden, culturally driven indicators that undermine world-class performance.

*The outcome of
this step of the
design process*

The outcome of this step in the design process—understanding the existing system—normally consists of three useful items: a feeling of the merits of the old system, a decision about reusing any of its infrastructure, and a set of performance indicators to bring forward into the next step of developing the detailed indicators for the new system.

7.4 UNDERSTANDING THE CURRENT PERFORMANCE MEASUREMENT SYSTEM AT PBI, I³M

The task at hand for the performance measurement design team was now to obtain an understanding of the current performance measurement system. The first thing the team did was to develop an internal questionnaire covering the most important issues.

The first question the team asked was what feelings the employees and management harbored for the existing system. In order to determine prevailing attitudes, team members met with a large number of people, including the CEO, another member of the management team, the union representative, and a few random middle managers and regular employees. After these separate meetings, the design team reassembled and concluded that management did not like the existing system at all. They felt they could never extract the data they wanted at any given time, and they generally did not trust the system.

The employees had a somewhat more positive attitude toward the system. However, they did feel that they had spent a lot of time entering numbers into the system. Although several employees did not see the true value of the system, others felt it was well functioning and producing the feedback they required. The team noticed that this, in particular, applied to the people working in customer complaints and procurement.

The team categorized the system as a formal one. The next step involved determining whether parts of the existing system infrastructure could be reused. First, the team assessed the routines and techniques for collecting data; then they reviewed the way data were analyzed, aggregated, and reported. For both issues, they looked into data quality and security as well as the resources required to perform these tasks. The first finding indicated that the routines for collecting data seemed inadequate for the amount of data collected. In addition, the team discovered that the ingoing data quality was questionable because the quality assurance system for collecting data seemed poor and the mechanisms for eliminating obvious errors were lacking. Therefore, they could understand some of the comments from management regarding their frustrations with the system.

The conclusions were more positive regarding how the data were analyzed, aggregated, and reported. The reporting templates in the old system were very useful, and some of them could be carried through to the new

STEP 3
Understanding the
Current Performance
Measurement System

system. The group also questioned whether the system was capable of offering support for improvement of the business processes. They concluded that the existing system did not contain features or enablers that enhanced an improvement focus, and that this issue should be addressed in the new system.

The final issue for the team consisted of sorting the existing performance indicators, based on a simple set of criteria. We will not bore you with listing the indicators placed in each category. Out of a total of 52 indicators, only seven fit into the "should be used" category. Nine indicators were on the "might be used" list, and the rest were not deemed appropriate for the new system.

Chapter 8

Step 4: Developing Performance Indicators

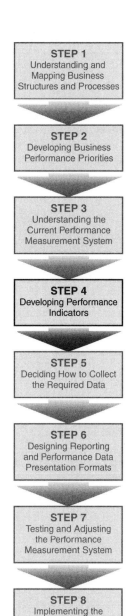

Your new state-of-the-art performance measurement system will consist of a number of elements, one of which is the set of performance indicators that you will use to measure the performance of your organization and its business processes. It is paramount that these indicators are designed with care. The surrounding infrastructure will enable the system to collect the data required to feed your instrument panel with the performance indicators, based on online and real-time data to the extent possible.

The development of performance indicators must be based on the business structure and process understanding and mapping from Step 1, as well as on the identified business performance priorities from Step 2. Performance indicator development should be completed for each business process, but in some cases processes might not be the suitable measurement object. Other measurement entities could be chosen. Indicators should be developed at both the process level and a higher organizational level. Some of these higher-level indicators might be aggregated from a lower level, while others only exist at the higher level. We will return to these issues later on in this chapter.

8.1 STEPS FOR DEVELOPING PERFORMANCE INDICATORS

Before we proceed to more detailed aspects of performance indicators, some generic substeps of this step of the system design process are:

STEP 4
Developing Performance
Indicators

Substeps for developing performance indicators

1. Establish who will be responsible for developing indicators for each business process—usually through design teams within smaller, confined areas—and any indicators required at a higher level of aggregation.

2. Teach the various indicator design teams how to develop performance indicators, including a review of characteristics of performance indicators.

3. Organize a brainstorming session to generate performance indicators. Utilize the guidelines provided in this chapter and abide by standard brainstorming rules—for example, no criticism allowed.

4. Define control limits and target values for each performance indicator (more about this very shortly).

5. Compile the resulting set of developed indicators from around the organization and different indicator design teams.

As we have already mentioned, the development of performance indicators is a highly creative process and typically the end result is extremely tailored to the specific needs of the organization. It would, therefore, be very presumptuous of us to try to provide you with generalized guidelines on how to go about this task. Instead, the bulk of this chapter consists of a run-through of some general issues to keep in mind when developing indicators for different types of business processes or other areas of the organization. Our main advice to the design team is to involve the people that know the processes in detail that are to be measured, and provide the best conditions for their creative sessions, for example, time off to do a proper job, adequate meeting rooms, perhaps a facilitator.

8.2 CONTROL LIMITS AND TARGET VALUES

We previously mentioned control limits and target values. Without going into a theoretical discussion about statistical process control (which deals with these matters more scientifically), it is often helpful to define these two concepts at this stage of the measurement system design process.

Control limit

A *control limit* is the lower level of accepted performance. Once the indicator passes below this limit, actions must be initiated. We do not use the plural term "limits" because the same logic does not apply at the other end of the scale. You want as high a performance as possible, thus you normally don't define an upper limit (although there might be situations where investing too much to raise a performance indicator of less importance to the overall success of the organization might result in misspent resources).

This leads us into the discussion of target values. A *target value* is, as the term implies, an agreed-upon target for the performance indicator. Attainment of this goal often lies some time in the future, in which case target timelines should also be defined. Again, the target value is not an upper limit of performance, but rather something to aim for in a reasonable time frame. If the indicator surpasses this target, nothing could be better, but then revised target values should be set.

We bring up these two concepts now, as it is logical to discuss them during the performance indicator definition work. The use of them will be further discussed in chapter 13.

STEP 4
Developing Performance
Indicators

Target value

8.3 DIFFERENT DIMENSIONS OF PERFORMANCE

When describing and measuring the performance level of a business process, a number of parameters might be relevant. It is pivotal to employ a balanced set of measures to understand the performance of the process and be able to locate improvement areas. Typical areas or types of performance measures to keep in mind are:

Typical features of performance indicators

- "Hard" versus "soft" measures

- Financial versus nonfinancial measures

- Result versus process measures

- Measures defined by their purpose—result, diagnostic, and competence

- Efficiency, effectiveness, and changeability

- The four classic measures (cost, time, quality, and flexibility)

It should be emphasized that, to a large extent, these features overlap, for example, the same measure might be categorized both as a "hard" and a result measure. We will now introduce the above-mentioned features, as well as other dimensions you should keep in mind in the development of performance indicators, for example, ethics and environmental issues.

The following sections will thus introduce these performance dimensions. Ideas for detailed performance indicators are listed in the appendix of this book. We would like to stress that these are examples and should not be used directly, but rather be adapted to suit the individual organization's characteristic features.

Detailed performance indicator examples are included in the appendix

STEP 4
Developing Performance
Indicators

Table 8.1   Differences between hard and soft measures

Hard Measures	Soft Measures
Objective reference	Observer bias
Accurately known	Surrogate indicator
Hierarchial	Multi-variable situation

"Hard" versus "Soft" Measures

Characteristics of hard and soft performance measures

Hard measures are pure facts that can be measured directly; soft measures are intangible measures that have to be measured indirectly. These are also known as quantitative and qualitative measures. A common problem is that you cannot directly measure the intended area, and in such cases you often need to resort to soft measures. Lead time is an example of a hard measure; customer satisfaction is a soft measure. Some differences between hard and soft measures are listed in Table 8.1.

Hard measures are most widely used by far, because soft measures are often viewed as so inaccurate that they are practically of no use at all. However, it has been claimed that the most important numbers are often unknown. Management by numbers is one of the deadly diseases that has ruined many enterprises in the Western world (Deming, 1986). Customer satisfaction is a good example of a performance measure that is basically a soft measure—best expressed as the customers' attitude toward the product or service being delivered. In fear of this being too difficult to measure accurately, many companies have tried to define customer satisfaction as the number of complaints or warranty costs. It is at best naïve, and at worst completely wrong to assume that those who do not complain are satisfied. The conclusion, in other words, is that both hard and soft measures are necessary to give a complete picture.

What makes soft measures difficult to use is that collecting such performance data can be troublesome or expensive. One approach is using surveys, which among others is explained in more detail in chapter 9.

Financial versus Nonfinancial Measures

Characteristics of financial performance measures

Financial measures include both direct and indirect measures involving monetary value as the measurement unit. Nonfinancial measures are a common denominator for performance indicators where the measurement unit is not monetary value. These can be both hard as well as soft. A few such measures are shown in Table 8.2.

Table 8.2 Examples of financial measures.

Financial Measure	Calculation (Simplified)
Profit margin	Total sales–total costs
Value added	Sales–input goods
Turnover of capital	Sales/total capital

Focusing on such financial measures is obviously an important part of the traditional way of running and managing a business. Financial measures are often viewed as synonymous with performance due to the direct link to the company's financial result.

As for hard and soft measures, the conclusion regarding financial and nonfinancial measures is that both are required. Problems arise when one of the categories is left out of the equation. Another issue related to financial and nonfinancial measures is green and blue savings:

*Green and
blue savings*

- Green savings are real cash savings visible in accounting systems, for example, layoffs and reduced purchase prices, overtime, and material usage. Real savings could be reinvested outside the company.

- Blue savings are indirect savings not necessarily visible in accounting, for example, reduced need for space, reduced lead-times, changed organizational culture, improved delivery rates, and improved product quality for the customer. These are internal savings or savings beneficial for the customers, not real cash savings that could be reinvested outside the company.

Investments in improvement projects often result in mainly blue savings. Green savings are usually difficult to achieve directly if performance is poor before the start of the project. This is especially true for small- and medium-sized organizations. Saving half a person is not a savings unless half of his or her salary is removed from the budget. The same argument could be used against idle space. International studies indicated that investments in modern manufacturing technology cannot be solely justified by traditional financial evaluation methods due to problems with transforming benefits into cash savings. Justification has to focus on performance improvement. Thus, economic evaluation methods are a necessary part of a more balanced approach, but should not be used alone, as we have already stressed on a number of occasions. Your performance measurement system should also be able to detect blue savings.

Results and process measures reflect the differences in management culture between Western and Eastern organizations

Result versus Process Measures

Result versus process measures are not necessarily conflicting concepts, but rather two types of measures that should also act in a balanced interplay. These two dimensions are, by the way, often used to illustrate the differences between Western and Japanese thinking when it comes to management. Western management culture emphasizes results and measures accordingly—by using measurement systems focused on measuring achievements.

In line with traditional Japanese attitudes, the most important part is performing the process in a respectable manner, which in turn will give the desired results. This is reflected in Japanese measurement systems, where far more emphasis is put on so-called process measures. *Process measures* are measures that describe certain important characteristics of a process that are assumed to have an effect on the desired results. An example could be the number of meetings held in a cross-functional team. The typical corresponding Western measure would be the number of changes implemented. Again, both types of measures have their place in a state-of-the-art performance measurement system.

Measures Defined According to Purpose

Three categories of performance measures

Performance measures can be classified according to the purpose of the measure—what they are supposed to say something about. Three common categories are:

1. Result measures

2. Diagnostic measures

3. Competence measures

Result measures

Result (achievement) measures indicate what the organization is achieving. These measures say something about what the organization has accomplished to this point, but they do not specify how this was achieved. They are quantitative and often financial. Some typical examples are net profit, return on investments, and market share.

Diagnostic measures

Diagnostic measures indicate probable future results. They are critical success factors for competition, and may be viewed as indirect indicators of achievement. The word *diagnostic* has the same meaning here as in healthcare—reaching a diagnosis for the process and prescribing a "cure" for it. Typical examples are delivery rates, delivery flexibility, product quality, lead times, and customer satisfaction.

Competence measures

Competence measures are the most difficult to define of the three. They should describe how well the organization is prepared to meet future

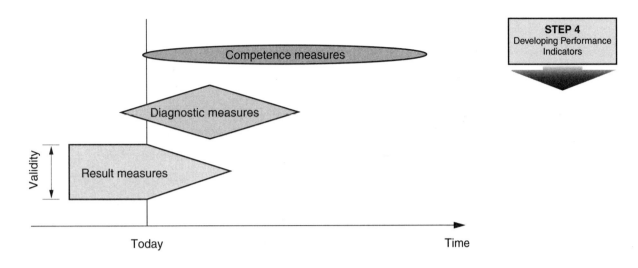

Figure 8.1　Validity horizon levels of the different measures.

requirements and challenges. Typical areas that ought to be addressed are complexity, competition, innovation, competence, training, and so on. Typical examples of competence measures are investments in product development, attitudes toward change, flexibility to manufacture totally new products or deliver totally new services, and training levels.

These three categories of measures have different validity levels. As depicted in Figure 8.1, result measures are most valid when discussing the past. Diagnostic measures are relevant for the immediate future; competence measures are generally hard to define in a way that offers high validity, but they should be able to say something about both the short- and long-term future.

8.4 PERFORMANCE INDICATORS FOR BUSINESS PROCESSES AND THE SUPPLY CHAIN

The previously described performance dimensions are generic, so other elements can be put to use in a number of processes. However, various processes have different characteristics on which to base the performance indicators. Throughout the next few sections, we will share some of our experiences when it comes to measuring detailed business processes. This will be based on a generic enterprise model, as illustrated in Figure 8.2.

A generic enterprise model

The process model consists of a number of business processes. The content of the processes will differ depending on the type of organization. A majority of the processes do, however, have common denominators in various organizations. The model consists of five types of processes/structures, in addition to the supply chain aspect:

Types of processes/structures

STEP 4
Developing Performance
Indicators

1. Primary processes, the value-adding processes commonly found in any organization, often labeled "main processes."

2. Secondary processes, processes supporting the execution of the primary processes. These are often labeled "support processes."

3. Development processes, processes aimed at improving the organization's performance, for instance new product/ service development.

4. Organizationwide characteristics, innate characteristics of the organization, for instance the external environment.

5. Stakeholders, the parties that can affect or are affected by the achievement of an organization's purpose. Please note that this is not a complete set of stakeholders, but rather a list of those related to the performance measurement system.

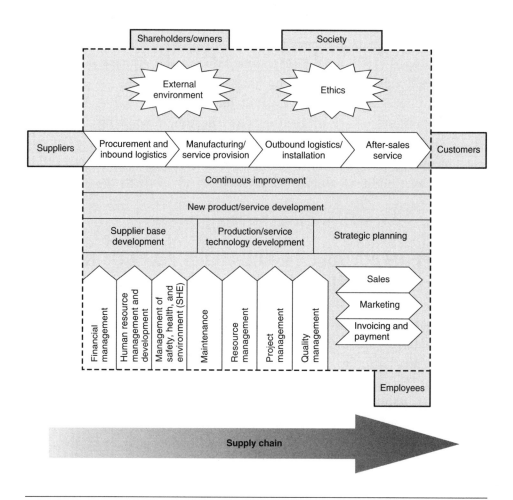

Figure 8.2 A generic process model.

The primary processes are depicted as arrows in the middle of the figure, starting with procurement and inbound logistics, and ending with after-sales service. In addition, three other primary processes are to be located a little further down in the figure (sales, marketing, and invoicing and payment).

The secondary processes are shown as arrows pointing upwards, illustrating a supportive approach. The development processes are presented as rectangles. Some of these cover the entire organization, like continuous improvement, whereas others are focused on a specific area, such as supplier base development.

The organizationwide characteristics are depicted as "clouds" in the upper part of the figure. Examples of structural factors are external environment and ethics. The dotted rectangle in the figure illustrates the boundaries of the organization. Outside these borders, a number of stakeholders operate, which are depicted as rectangles. The model also illustrates that the organization should seek to satisfy each stakeholder.

We will now address each of the processes in the model and what you should remember when developing performance indicators for that process. In addition, you should always try to keep in mind the generic performance characteristics previously described when developing performance indicators.

The thoroughness of the explanation will vary for the different processes, both due to varying complexity and the extent of relevant performance indicators available, for example, there are fewer good operational performance indicators for strategic planning compared to manufacturing and service provision.

8.5 PRIMARY PROCESSES

Characteristics of primary processes

The most common primary processes are procurement and inbound logistics, manufacturing/service provision, outbound logistics/installation, after-sales service, sales, marketing, and invoicing and payment. The content of each process will differ depending on the type of enterprise (for example, service or manufacturing) and its core business. A radio station and a travel agent will have quite different primary processes, even though both are service-providing companies. In addition, some companies have outsourced parts of their processes, for example, invoicing and payment, making the picture even more complicated. Therefore, it is essential to determine which processes the organization actually performs (and how), not just pick standard ones from a list of common processes.

What are the characteristics of primary processes? First of all, it is common that vast amounts of data regarding these processes can be found in the

STEP 4
Developing Performance
Indicators

organization's various computer systems. Whenever large amounts of data are gathered, it is always important to question their accuracy. If you cannot trust the source data, the performance indicators will not be very dependable either. If you are satisfied that data are correct, the challenge is to select the right performance indicators. As we have stressed a number of times, the set of performance indicators must be balanced, enabling a holistic picture of the performance of the process. In this process, the different performance dimensions described earlier in this chapter can be of help.

While it is important to find valid performance indicators for each primary process, because they are interlinked and dependent upon each other, it is also important to avoid suboptimizing the different processes. There are, basically, at least two things you can do to avoid this. First of all, you should compare the selected performance indicators from all of the primary processes in order to end up with a balanced set. In addition, so-called end-to-end performance indicators for entire value chains of primary processes help extend the unit of analysis beyond single business processes.

While we will not devote much space to it, poor quality cost measurements deserve mentioning. This is almost a field of its own devoted to measuring the negative effects, in monetary values, of every activity deviating from the norm. If an error is made during assembly of a product and parts must be scrapped, this causes poor quality costs in the amount of the value of the ruined parts and the time wasted on reassembly. If a service delivery process fails and leaves the customer frustrated, poor quality costs are incurred in terms of time wasted for a service that must be delivered over again and loss of goodwill from that customer. The point of these kinds of measurements is to convert all such negative effects into "money language" to use them as an indicator of the organization's performance level. Poor quality cost measurements have their merits and can be one approach to measuring performance of both primary, support, and development processes.

8.6 SECONDARY PROCESSES

Secondary processes are not as uniform and streamlined as primary processes, but rather are a collection of different processes all aimed at supporting and enhancing the execution of the primary ones. Typical secondary processes are financial management; human resource management and development; management of safety, health, and environment (internal environment); resource management; project management; and quality management. Some of these might be labeled management processes, whereas others are more focused on control and preventive actions.

A common trait in most secondary processes, however, is that they consist of variables that are not normative—if you measure an indicator labeled "resources used for maintenance," then there is no "right" level for this indicator. The answer is neither zero nor a very high number, but somewhere in between. Creating performance indicators under such conditions will often demand a certain creativity to help find the right result.

Is it less important to measure secondary processes than primary ones? Our answer is a definite "no." Support processes play an important part in any organization. There is also a parallel to the difference between result measures and process measures. At an aggregated level, performance indicators for the secondary processes can be viewed as the process measures for the company, while many of the performance measures for the primary processes can be viewed as result measures. As you will remember, you need both.

Support process performance indicators are rarely normative

8.7 DEVELOPMENT PROCESSES

The magnitude and diversity of development processes in an organization will depend on its type of business and which phase it is in. Common development processes are continuous improvement, new product/service development, supplier base development, production/service technology development, and strategic planning.

Development processes' performance can be difficult to isolate from effects of other activities in the organization

What are typical traits of development processes? In our experience, it might be hard to define the exact goals of some of the development processes, for example, a continuous improvement process or product/service development. With a "moving target," that is a process constantly changing, defining performance indicators also becomes more difficult. Furthermore, there are few normative aspects of these processes—it is absurd to claim that as much as possible should be invested in training or at least 15 percent of revenues should be channeled into product development.

Another characteristic of development processes is that the time delay between action and response is often longer than in other types of processes. This is certainly a challenge when measuring performance. Another related issue is that with such a time delay, it might also be difficult to isolate the effects of a process, as the level of disturbance will be high. A performance indicator capturing the improvement in time-to-market for new products will be affected by both the new product development process and several other activities in the organization.

There is often a time lag between when a development process is executed and the result can be measured

The development processes are not standardized, so it is hard to define a best practice or reference model. The same argument applies to target values for the performance indicators. Earlier we talked about blue and green

STEP 4
Developing Performance
Indicators

savings; many development processes contribute more to blue savings than to green. Therefore, it is important to also develop performance indicators that focus on these savings.

8.8 ORGANIZATIONWIDE CHARACTERISTICS

Any organization will have a number of organizationwide characteristics. However, many of these are not relevant in a performance measurement context, for example, organizational architecture. We have, therefore, only included the external environment and ethics characteristics. External environment, and the "green" focus in general, has been a hot topic the last few years, and as such is important to include in your state-of-the-art measurement system. Ethics is a relatively new issue, but has a strong momentum. We think that ethical aspects will become pivotal to performance in the near future.

External Environment

Environmental awareness is rapidly increasing in all groups of society

Environmental awareness is probably the single general public interest topic that is growing most rapidly, especially in industrialized countries. Simply by looking at media attention to this issue, we can easily infer what level of importance the average human being attaches to environmental impacts caused by an organization. Some trends that can currently be clearly identified are:

- The number of members/financial contributors of various environmental preservation societies and associations is increasing dramatically.

- While members of these institutions (especially young people) used to be well to the left in terms of political preferences, people from all ages and walks of life are now drawn to these organizations.

- The amount of legislation related to environmental protection has exploded during the last few years, both nationally and internationally, for example, EU, UN, and so on.

- The number of recycling and reuse schemes, both in industry and privately, is on the rise, and most people engage in one or more such programs.

- Unnatural climatic effects suspected to stem from pollution have increased and receive much media attention, for example, global warming, more frequent tropical storms, smog, and so on.

What consequences do these developments have on the individual enterprise and the ways in which it seeks to achieve competitiveness? A simplified answer is that the effects materialize at two main levels. First of all, failure to comply with existing legislation can lead to economic penalties—fees and fines. These will impact competitiveness through increased costs, which then must be recovered through higher prices or suffering lower profitability. Second, and much more important, the increasingly conscious customer wants environmentally sound products and has an amazing ability to discover any conduct that contributes to damaging the environment. A high and ever-growing number of customers demand clean products and are even willing to pay more, accept less comfort or fewer features, or wait longer if a product is believed to be more beneficial to the environment.

Therefore, it is becoming increasingly more important for an enterprise to be able to manage its operations in a way that minimizes negative environmental impact, directly or indirectly. When combining the pivotal importance of environmental friendliness with the need for performance measurement, it is evident that "green performance measurement" is crucial and something every enterprise should master.

Some important principles in the area of environmental management are: prevention of waste by technologies and products, recycling and reuse, optimization of final disposal, regulation of transport, and remedial action. If we wish to assess a product's environmental damage, all lifecycle phases must be studied. Figure 8.3 helps to understand a product's lifecycle, illustrating its inputs and outputs.

Both generic principles and the lifecycle view should be kept in mind when developing environmental performance indicators. It can be useful to

Consequences for organizations of increased environmental concern

Areas of environmental concern

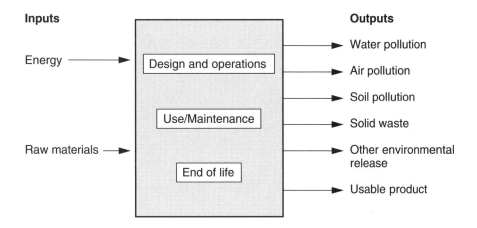

Figure 8.3 Inputs and outputs of a product over its lifecycle.

STEP 4
Developing Performance
Indicators

*Categories into
which environmental
impact performance
indicators can
be sorted*

sort proposed indicators into suitable categories while they are being developed. We suggest the following:

- Design area. This category focuses on the design process and is intended to influence the environmental effects of the product from its conception. These indicators are based on legislative requirements and requirements of end-of-life disposition methods.

- Operations area. Operational performance indicators provide information about the environmental performance of the organization's operations.

- Use area. Use performance indicators provide information about the product during its use phase.

- End-of-life area. This category focuses on the end-of-life phase of the product. These indicators are influenced by proposed and existing legislation, for example, prescribed minimum recycling rates for electronic and electrical goods as well as automotives.

- Management area. Whereas other environmental indicator categories provide an indication of the present state of a company's environmental performance, management indicators furnish information on steps taken to influence operations. Management indicators provide information on managers' efforts to improve an organization's environmental performance and are useful in the quantification of environmental management targets. Management indicators describe such things as the allocation of funds and labor, implementation of environmental programs and new environmental policies, environmentally related legal expenses, environmental remediation activities, and the status of environmental information systems.

What environmental performance indicators should be employed by your organization? In the Appendix, we have provided some examples of performance indicators. However, as for the other areas mentioned in this book, we urge you to develop your own performance indicators based on the situation of your organization. The indicators in the Appendix can then be used as examples.

Ethics

*Personal and
corporate greed*

Throughout recent history, it might seem as if personal and corporate greed have been increasing to become the most prominent feature of today's society. Individuals spend more and more time working, to earn more money to pay for more, larger, and better housing, cars, appliances, clothes, travel,

STEP 4
Developing Performance
Indicators

and so on. Traditional family values are deteriorating, resulting in broken homes, single-parent families, and so on, with further pressure to keep working longer hours to compensate for the lost income. Results can be seen in terms of increased drug abuse, elevated crime levels, and serious juvenile problems.

Correspondingly, the governmental part of society has grown more concerned with financial resources—having to provide more services with less money. Again, results manifest themselves in a colder society that offers less "positive" services to its citizens and spends more and more on "negative" services like judicial, police, and punishment systems. Finally, the corporate world displays perhaps the most extreme signs of this greedy trait. The main and foremost objective for any commercial organization is to maximize its profits. Most modern organizations realize that in order to survive in today's competitive arena, customers have to be satisfied. However, profits are higher when more money can be charged for less value. Anyone who has bought something that has broken within the warranty period knows what a struggle it can be to have it repaired or replaced at no extra cost.

The real-time focus enhanced by TV, radio, and the Internet increases the focus on ethical issues

Furthermore, most people know that high-level industrial managers make a shameful amount of money, both in direct salaries and in terms of bonuses and stock options. In addition, scandals are disclosed weekly about inside stock trading, additional generous compensation schemes, favorable retirement plans, and so on, all while these same managers continue to advocate downsizing and fight unions over any pay raise. Lastly, the real-time focus enhanced by TV, radio, and the Internet increases the focus on ethical issues, as the downside of unethical behavior can be distributed worldwide within minutes, for example, issues regarding child labor, discrimination, and pollution.

Customer uncertainty

Of course, this is a very black-and-white picture emphasizing the grim aspects of modern society. Still, no one really disputes that a current general trait is personal and corporate ego-centered profit maximization. From a customer's point of view, this usually results in a general uncertainty as to whether he or she received a bargain or was taken totally by the nose. In order to come up with a competitive offer, a company must offer high value at a low price. At the same time, this company must charge as high a price as possible for as little material and effort put into the product or service as possible. As customers cannot know which of these conflicting pressures dominates a given situation, they cannot feel certain that the deal was beneficial for them. Did I pay too much? Is the quality poor? Did the manufacturer use inferior components to save a few dollars? Am I paying for the CEO's next Mercedes? Will my money in turn be used to clear away some square meters of rain forest for the next project the company gets engaged in? And so on.

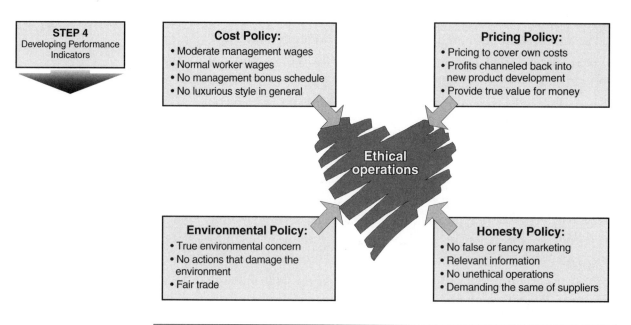

Figure 8.4   Ethical operations.

Ethical policies that can be exploited for performance measurement of ethical aspects

Thus, the customer's uncertainty following a purchase might be related to cost, value, and quality issues, but in a larger context this could be an ethical topic. In comparison with this trend, there is a general, growing business ethics movement that has created the new position of "ethics officer." Certainly there is no standard recipe on how to become ethical or how to measure the degree of ethical behavior. In Figure 8.4 we have, however, tried to give an overview of what ethical operations *could* entail (the word "could" was chosen deliberately).

These policies represent one way of measuring the ethical aspects of your operations, but there are certainly others as well. The problem we find with the ethical aspect of business is that there are many "big words" used to discuss the topic, but very little is available in terms of an operative interpretation of the term. If you come across any good performance indicators for this area, please let us know!

8.9 STAKEHOLDERS

Measure both your ability to satisfy your stakeholders and their ability to satisfy you

Stakeholders are the parties that can affect or are affected by the achievement of your organization's performance. We have included the following stakeholders in this model: suppliers, shareholders/owners, society, customers, and employees. However, for many organizations, other stakeholders might apply—the media or environmental pressure groups. You should normally measure your ability to satisfy the stakeholders' demands *and* performance by satisfying your own. When developing indicators, you should also keep in mind that it is not always the best strategy to satisfy all stakeholders' demands by 100 percent. If you jump every time a stakeholder tells you to, you will do a lot of bouncing. It does not follow that you should not measure your performance toward the stakeholders; rather that target values for the indicators should be set at reasonable levels, with a holistic focus in mind.

Product or service performance measurement

For all stakeholders in the organization's environment, it is possible to construe the relationship with them as an exchange of products or services (if funding, information, and so on is seen as a product or service). The reason for this rather unusual view is that we want to set the stage for pointing out the importance of measuring the performance of your products or services. These are the most obvious outputs you deliver to the surroundings, and there is a long history for measuring aspects of product or service performance. From this fact, it is logical that large numbers of well-defined performance indicators have been developed, and this is something you should take advantage of when developing your own indicators.

Some stakeholder performance data must be gathered from outside your own organization

When trying to measure your ability to satisfy the stakeholders, some of the required data can be found inside your own organization, for example, delivery rates for your customers. These indicators will not tell the whole truth, though. In many cases, you will need to perform some sort of a survey of more subjective views on the part of the stakeholders—for example, customer satisfaction surveys—and feed these data into the performance measurement system manually.

When dealing with performance indicators for the stakeholders' performance, we should also discuss the degree of openness between the organization and its stakeholders. In many cases, it is favorable for the development of the relationship to have an open attitude and discuss both the definition of the indicators as well as their levels and trends. This is dependent on your use of indicators for improvement rather than for control or sanctions!

8.10 THE SUPPLY CHAIN

Supply chains are becoming increasingly important in the modern business world

Supply chains are becoming increasingly important in the modern business world. In many cases, the competition is becoming a battle between supply chains instead of between individual companies. It is thus of vital importance to be a member of the right supply chains and to streamline them for survival and prosperity. In a supply chain, openness is the key to enhancing performance along the chain. In an open cooperation, you should share performance data with suppliers upstream (first- and higher-tier suppliers) and customers downstream (first- and higher-tier customers) to put focus

STEP 4
Developing Performance
Indicators

*Performance data
openness along
supply chains*

on improvement of the chain as a whole, as this creates a win-win situation for all members. To allow comparison of performance indicators, it is usually worthwhile to standardize the indicators that are to be studied.

This leads us into a discussion about data openness and data systems. To streamline performance along a supply chain, you might want to consider having a common performance measurement layer for the chain. This layer could upload performance data to a common database or Web site (the openness and access rights of this database or Web site would be topic for discussion). If a supply chain consists of companies A, B, C, and D, one option might be that company C could only access the data related to its interface with companies B and D. Another option could be whether all data or just key data were open to the entire supply chain. Such an option is based on an atmosphere of trust among the participants.

Another aspect of supply chain measurement is aggregation of performance indicators to overall indicators for the whole chain. When aggregating in this manner, it is important to ensure that the aggregated indicators are still valid and unambiguous. We have seen many aggregated indicators that have little or no meaning.

*Supply chain
performance
measurement for
supply chain
composition*

A few last words about the applications of supply chain performance measurement versus single-organization measurement. The two are similar in their use for performance development monitoring and improvement (both the identification of where to improve and after-the-fact follow-up). However, an extra dimension in the supply chain measurement is that the performance data can be used to compose and recompose supply chains. Even though many supply chains remain stable for long periods of time, others go through frequent redesigns by replacing links in the chain with new ones that perform better. Supply chain performance measurement offers fact-based support for this objective by allowing insight into where performance levels are and are not satisfactory. A last word of warning, though: since supply chain performance measurement makes available the continuously updated performance data, consider using the information to make the weaker links realize their need for improvement and give them a second chance before they are thrown out. Integrating new members into the chain requires time and investments!

8.11 RELATED CONCEPTS

We have provided some guidelines on developing performance indicators for the processes in a typical organization. At the end of this chapter, we want to present two related concepts that we feel deserve inclusion in this book, but which we have been unable to insert anywhere else: balanced scorecard and performance in "the new economy." *Balanced scorecard* is a fairly new approach for performance measurement that promotes many of the same core principles as we do, for example, measurement of several dimensions of performance, performance measurement for early warning, and so on. In balanced scorecard, however, the framework for what should be measured is somewhat more rigid than what we advocate and restricted to the measurement areas prescribed. Balanced scorecard is currently being used in a number of enterprises worldwide, and you should thus be familiar with the concept. Finally, we want to present some ideas regarding the new economy and how it can be subjected to performance measurement.

The Balanced Scorecard Approach

Balanced scorecard is an example of a predefined performance measurement system. The origins of balanced scorecard can be traced back to 1990 when the Nolan Norton Institute sponsored a one-year multicompany study labeled "Measuring Performance in the Organization of the Future." The study was motivated by the belief that existing performance measurement approaches, primarily relying on financial accounting measures, were becoming obsolete. The study participants felt that "reliance on summary financial performance measures was hindering the organizations' abilities to create future economic value" (Kaplan and Norton, 1996). Recent case studies of innovative performance measurement systems were examined early in the project. One case study demonstrated how a company utilized a newly created "corporate scorecard." Following discussions in the study group the scorecard was expanded to what they have now labeled a "balanced scorecard." Several of the participants experimented with building prototypes of balanced scorecards.

"Reliance on summary financial performance measures was hindering the organizations' abilities to create future economic value"

Kaplan and Norton argued that financial measures only tell the story of the past, and that they are inadequate for guiding and evaluating the journey that information age companies must make. Kaplan and Norton stated: "The balanced scorecard complements financial measures of past performance with measures of drivers of future performance. The objectives and measures of the scorecard are derived from an organization's vision and strategy. The objectives and measures view organizational performance from four perspectives: financial, customer, internal business process, and learning and growth. These four perspectives provide the framework for the balanced scorecard."

The purpose of the balanced scorecard is thus to develop an organization-specific balanced scorecard to monitor and guide the organization's evolution. The balanced scorecard approach involves translating the organization's

The purpose of balanced scorecard is thus to develop an organization-specific balanced scorecard to monitor and guide the organization's evolution

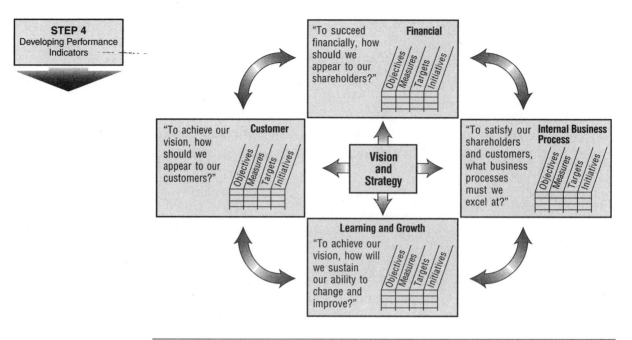

Figure 8.5 The balanced scoreboard.

strategy into tangible objectives and measures. The framework for the balanced scorecard can be seen in Figure 8.5.

According to Kaplan and Norton, the measures are balanced between:

The balanced scorecard aims to strike a balance between: external versus internal measures, outcome versus performance-driving measures, and quantifiable versus subjective measures

1. External measures for shareholders and customers and internal measures for critical business processes, innovation, and a learning culture.

2. Outcome measures and measures that drive performance.

3. Objective, easily quantified outcome measures and subjective, somewhat judgmental performance drivers for the outcome measures.

In our opinion, there are several ways of using the balanced scorecard when developing your performance measurement system. The balanced scorecard can be employed as a reference model or its indicators can be used as examples and facilitators in the creative development process.

Performance Indicators in the New Economy

Manufacturing of goods in traditional high cost regions such as the United States, Europe, and so on, is a topic about which many arguments are raised, both pro and con. No matter what position you take, it is a fact that the economies of these regions are changing. Knowledge enterprises constitute an ever-increasing portion of employment and economic activity, while at the same time knowledge generation is a prerequisite for maintaining traditional manufacturing industries. The terms *the old* and *the new,* not to mention *the new new,* economies are in frequent use today, although without a precise definition of their meaning. Some have, however, pointed out that the new economy is global; favors less tangible concepts like ideas, information, and relationships; and is extremely interconnected. Western industry must obviously follow along in the development of "the new economy" and knowledge-intensive activities, but in a manner that secures a solid foundation for long-term survival, viability, and employment.

The "new" and the "new new" economy

With the evolution of the new economy during the last few years, we have seen a type of organization emerge that obviously does not abide by the established norms for financial status, assessment of market potential, customer satisfaction, and so on. Apparently this part of industry lives by its own set of rules, where investors make completely different valuations than what is common in investment analyses for traditional enterprises. In the new economy, companies seem to accept the outline conditions of years of low revenues and income in lieu of a market potential that they believe exists, and where facade and presentation toward the market seem to be more important, at least for a certain phase, than a real ability to deliver products or services. In addition, a specific common trait of these enterprises is that their rapid growth—in terms of revenue, value, and employees—does not leave them the time to develop the systems, routines, support staff, and so on that are required in organizations of a certain size.

Some companies seem to live by different rules than others

At the same time, an adjustment has occurred among investors in their attitudes toward the types of enterprises and ventures where extremely inflated stock rates have fallen significantly and large Internet-based companies struggle with liquidity and credibility, for example, amazon.com, letsbuyit.com, and so on. The first bankruptcies in the new economy have occurred (boo.com, dressmart.com, toysmart.com, and so on), and in their wake, a somewhat disturbing state of affairs has been disclosed regarding real customer attraction abilities, delivery, income, and financial position. Still, there is nothing to indicate that the new economy cannot become a major source for employment, especially in Western countries with negative competitive advantage in terms of wage levels for physical manufacturing of products. A source for improved long-term viability for this type of company might be the development of performance measurement principles and systems suited to the new economy.

Much of the new economy sector has faced severe problems lately

Consequently, a new approach to this subject is needed. Proposals have been made as to how to shape a new approach , but they focus primarily on evaluating organizations where a large portion of their value consists of

New approaches for performance measurement in new economy enterprises are required

so-called intangible assets— knowledge, brand names, distribution channels, and so on. The focus of this evaluation has been on traditional accounting's lack of ability to capture such intangible values, which is counterproductive in the type of companies that make up the new economy. So far, little has been done regarding the application of operational performance measures in the new economy. For example, many Internet-based stores that have struggled financially during the last few years have been criticized for putting all their efforts into professional Web pages, while failing to develop a logistics machinery on the same level. The result has been either extreme costs related to very large inventories or unacceptably long delivery times for customers.

If these companies had established a balanced performance measurement system to encourage the development of both Web pages and the logistics system, such failures could have been avoided. Implementing suitable performance measures that promote the aspects required for the survival of this kind of organization can, therefore, become an important mechanism to ensure a balanced development for organizations of the new economy.

8.12 DEVELOPING PERFORMANCE INDICATORS IN PBI, I³M

In Step 3, the performance measurement design team had reviewed the existing performance indicators and found a few worth keeping, and now the team was prepared to populate the business process model with detailed indicators. Having done a thorough job in the previous steps, they felt ready to begin.

First, they had to decide who would develop the indicators for each of the 22 processes. One extreme approach would have 22 different groups for designing indicators, while the other extreme would have the design team or another group do all the work. The team did not feel comfortable with either of these options. Although the former would ensure the involvement of a large number of people, it would require a great deal of resources and the expected consistency in the resulting indicators would be questionable. In the latter approach, the team felt it did not have enough in-depth knowledge about all the processes to design the indicators themselves. In addition, the user-participation would be very limited.

The design team decided on a middle course. They clustered processes together and formed a development group for each cluster. Some clusters only consisted of two processes—for example, customer commitment and

sales and market development, while other clusters were composed of many processes—for example, operations.

The development groups were then trained in the development and different characteristics of performance indicators. For practical purposes, the design team and the development groups gathered at a hotel for two half-day sessions. By removing people from the organization, they were able to focus on the task at hand and align their thinking toward performance indicators throughout the business processes.

One week after the hotel session, each group met to have brainstorming sessions. One member of the design team was present in all brainstorming sessions to act as facilitator and ensure consistency. This member tried to remind the group of the different performance dimensions and to come up with indicators covering the "missing" dimensions. Each brainstorming session lasted two to three hours. For those with many processes, a whole day was allocated.

After each session, the preliminary results were listed and distributed to the participants. For some of the clusters, a second session was needed to finish up and ensure consistency. For each of the 22 processes, the result was a list of accepted performance indicators. We will not present this list here, but to give you an idea of indicators suggested for an operations process, the following examples are quite typical:

- Availability of the system

- Percentage of operation activities executed according to plan

- Percentage of time used for preventive maintenance as opposed to corrective maintenance

- Average time between alarm occurrence and resolution of alarm cause

- Average operation cost per system or service

Chapter 9

Step 5: Deciding How to Collect the Required Data

STEP 1
Understanding and
Mapping Business
Structures and Processes

STEP 2
Developing Business
Performance Priorities

STEP 3
Understanding the
Current Performance
Measurement System

STEP 4
Developing Performance
Indicators

STEP 5
Deciding How to Collect
the Required Data

STEP 6
Designing Reporting
and Performance Data
Presentation Formats

STEP 7
Testing and Adjusting
the Performance
Measurement System

STEP 8
Implementing the
Performance
Measurement System

A major task in the performance measurement system design process is the definition of the performance indicators, as these will constitute the actual contents of the measurement system. However, a performance measurement system is only as good as the performance data it is ultimately able to present to users. Defining a multitude of smart and fancy indicators is, in the end, of no use if your system is incapable of collecting the data required to compile those indicators, and do so accurately and in a timely fashion. Thus, much care should be put into the development of the data collection mechanisms of your state-of-the-art performance measurement system, which is the topic of this chapter.

We should also point out that the sequential presentation of the steps, as must be presented in book format, could be slightly inaccurate in this phase of the development process. Intuitively, it would be foolish to complete the step of performance indicator development without any thought about whether it is possible to, or precisely how to, collect the performance data these indicators will require, and then move on to try to find ways of overcoming the data requirements. If you are aiming for a computer-based performance measurement system (more about this shortly), then the same also goes for the ensuing step of designing reporting and performance data presentation formats. These three steps must, to some extent, be treated simultaneously to make sure that requirements posed by one step can be fulfilled by the next. In this book, however, we will treat them in sequence and urge you to make sure you achieve consistency across these two or three steps.

Some important issues that the performance measurement system design team must address in this step are:

STEP 5
Deciding How to Collect
the Required Data

Performance measurement system design issues related to performance data collection

- Data availability

- Production costs for producing the required performance data

- Data accuracy

- The data collection approach

- Data collection responsibility

- The frequency of measurement and data collection

- Storage of the performance data

As you can probably tell, this is not a step-by-step checklist, but it is a somewhat unsorted set of topics that you need to think through in connection with performance data collection. We will try to provide you with some guidance for each of these issues.

9.1 DATA AVAILABILITY, COST, AND ACCURACY

Electronic data are a good starting point

In our experience, there is almost no end to the amount of data most companies record and store in different ways. There is also no guarantee that you will have access to the specific performance data required to calculate all of the intriguing indicators you would like to measure. Taking stock of what data is actually available is, therefore, an important task. If you can find a repository of data already containing what you are looking for, this is certainly the best way to collect your data. In this day and age, where most of the various functions of organizations have been transferred from manually recorded paper ledgers into computer systems, chances are actually quite good that you might find what you need already "lying around" somewhere. Such data, collected and stored electronically, are by far the best performance data to use in your measurement system, so this is where you should start your data search. Do keep in mind, however, that such electronic data must be regularly updated to be of any use to you!

ERP systems are a very good data source

Typically, electronic databases contain a lot of the "bean counter" data that you need, for example, any possible type of cost data, resource usage, inventory levels, order data, times, and so on. Accounting systems, human resource management systems, order tracking systems, planning systems, and so on, contain massive amounts of this kind of information, and they are normally updated very frequently. The latest fad in enterprise IT systems is, of course, the infamous enterprise resource planning (ERP) systems that have flourished during the last few years, for example, SAP, Oracle, BaaN, Great Plains, and so on. These typically integrate and replace a number of previously isolated systems containing typical fact-based data. If your organization uses one of these systems, chances are that this is where you will find a great deal of your needed "bean counting."

However, if you have already tried your hand at defining performance indicators for some of the softer areas— environmental impact, customer satisfaction, or business ethics—we highly doubt that you will find your required performance data for these types of indicators within your ERP system, or any other IT system for that matter. These are typically the kind of data that need to be specifically collected for the performance measurement system, and are thus normally more difficult and costly to obtain. On the other hand, these performance dimensions are often as—if not more—important than the fact-based dimensions. Not including them in the performance measurement system simply because it is harder to collect the data is, therefore, not a very wise decision.

There are, however, some ways to overcome this problem. Of course, the most obvious is to accept the time, trouble, and costs involved in collecting these data, whether through customer surveys, manual measurement and data collection, or some other approach. If you deem these performance data crucial, this is probably worthwhile. Surveys are nearly a science unto themselves, and we will not go into details about them here. They can provide a very rich information set from a large number of sources, but they can be so expensive that perhaps it is only feasible for you to conduct one per year.

Another approach is to look for substitute data that, if not equally as good as the intended data, can at least be an acceptable replacement. Measuring facts in areas of a softer nature is normally more costly than using a subjective method, such as evaluations based on judgment, surveys, or surrogate indicators. Such substitutes for hard data will usually be less accurate, but this must be decided based on costs, whether hard data are available at all, and the importance of the indicator. Further, validity requirements of a metric also depend on its purpose and use. If the primary purpose is to monitor the *trend* of the metric, somewhat less accurate measurement approaches can be perfectly acceptable.

"Surrogate indicators" often require a creative definition, but can be very good alternatives to the original hard indicator. Say that you want to measure customer satisfaction but find that conducting frequent surveys of a large number of customers will be too expensive. If you are able to record the names of your customers—you have a closer customer relationship than over-the-counter cash transactions—then measuring the repeat purchasing customer frequency can be an acceptable substitute. Some indicators might be so loosely defined that they are almost impossible to measure, for example, the "suitability of the product development team's areas in terms of

STEP 5
Deciding How to Collect
the Required Data

Softer performance data are rarely available in computer systems

Surrogate indicators

STEP 5
Deciding How to Collect
the Required Data

Data collection from external sources

ability to stimulate creativity" (which is an actual indicator that one of our clients asked us to help them implement). Since there are obviously no hard facts revealing this information—we tried looking into the issues of air quality, colors, the availability of different types of furniture and equipment, and so on—the best answer is probably a strikingly obvious surrogate indicator: recording the trend in the number of new product ideas launched, innovations produced, or sales from new products as a percentage of total revenues. While these obviously are impacted by many other factors in the organization, they are also certainly connected to what we wanted to measure. But beware of surrogates that are too far-fetched and less capable of acting as true surrogates than what you had hoped for!

For some indicators, you will have to depend on data sources that are external to your own organization, for example customers, suppliers, and partners. According to the rationale of the stakeholder model and the mutual influence between you and your stakeholders, it might be wise to try to develop closer relationships to these sources in order to obtain data from them. If you can convince them that it is in their best interest for your organization to perform at its best, then they probably will not mind supplying you with relevant data for your performance measurement system, especially if the data are readily available or not very complicated to generate.

9.2 ACTUAL DATA COLLECTION

From our work with performance measurement systems, we have come to realize that there are basically only four different ways of collecting performance data:

1. From previously collected repositories of electronically stored data, to which access can be facilitated through electronic means—by querying a database, having a file transferred, getting data exported from a software application, or in some other way that is available to the performance measurement system.

2. From previously collected repositories of data stored on paper, meaning that some kind of manual operation must be performed to gather the data and make them available for the performance measurement system.

3. By setting up a new mechanism for capturing data electronically, for example, by setting up a bar code registration application or by having employees record in a spreadsheet the time spent on certain tasks.

4. By manually recording the required data and entering them into the performance measurement system. In this manner, the manual recording can take the form of measuring physical dimensions using a tape measure, measuring time using a clock, reading a gage at certain time intervals, asking suppliers to rate the accuracy of your purchase orders, and so on.

STEP 5
Deciding How to Collect
the Required Data

Very often, these approaches also correlate with the cost and time requirements of collecting data—simply extracting electronic data from a readily available database is the cheapest and fastest way, while running around actually measuring this and that is the most expensive way and takes the longest amount of time. Although there are numerous examples to the contrary, the same often holds true for the accuracy of the data.

We recommend that you try to accomplish your data collection in the indicated order. Start by looking for already existing electronic data. It will be terrific if you find some, but if you don't, then see if some data have been collected that can either be used instead or converted to what you are looking for. This often requires the help and insight of the organization's IT system guru, and this person might even be a logical member of the design team at this stage of the process. On many occasions, we included such people in the creative discussions about performance indicators and data availability and consequently gained a lot from their presence. They are also invaluable help if you need to resort to the third option—implementing some type of electronic data collection mechanism.

IT staff are a positive supplement to the performance measurement system design team

9.3 MANUAL OR ELECTRONIC PERFORMANCE MEASUREMENT SYSTEMS

An issue from the beginning of this chapter that we have been very unsure how to handle is the question of what will constitute the infrastructure of your performance measurement system. Have you given this any thought so far, or perhaps you automatically conjured up an image of the system from the very outset? Depending on which "implementation mode" you choose, much of the discussion regarding data collection approaches can take on two connotations.

In our view, there are basically two archetypes of performance measurement systems—manual or electronic. Unfortunately, the distinction between the two can at times be less than perfectly obvious! When we began working with performance measurement and performance measurement systems, the main objective was to supply top management with more extensive and diverse data for decision-making support than

STEP 5
Deciding How to Collect
the Required Data

the traditional accounting reports they would receive now and then. The objective was met by having someone in the organization collect the necessary performance data and compile a report that was frequently a printout, but sometimes a spreadsheet or word processing file. This person, however, would almost exclusively record and store the underlying data in a spreadsheet file or some other electronic format. Would you call this a manual or electronic performance measurement system? What if all the performance data are stored in an electronic database accessible by every employee of the organization, but a fairly large amount of the underlying performance data is collected by hand? To be a little more precise, we will employ the following definitions of manual and electronic performance measurement systems:

System type definitions

- In a manual performance measurement system, performance data are accessed and presented on paper in the form of a printed report.

- In an electronic performance measurement system, performance data are typically accessible from PCs or computer terminals scattered around the organization and presented on screen to the user.

As you can see, these are not very precise definitions—and there probably is no need for them either. It is almost impossible to imagine someone running a performance measurement system based on recording and storing the performance data on paper instead of a computer. It is almost inconceivable that none of the performance data used in the system stem from electronic sources of some sort, no matter how small the organization might be. However, there is an important distinction between the more cumbersome types of systems, where the performance data is extracted only when needed and the performance indicators are presented on paper to a select group of target users, and the modern performance measurement systems based on online access to a continuously updated database of performance data. The former is an old-fashioned type of system that, although certainly much better than having no system at all, is being made obsolete by the latter type, which is much more powerful and user-friendly. And contrary to what you might think, the electronic type is not necessarily more expensive. You can get quite far with some basic insight into the most common office software applications and Web site design tools, which are usually much easier and cheaper to run and maintain than manual systems. Lately, there are even some commercial offerings available for customizing a system to your organization's needs, which can further reduce the limitations of such systems.

9.4 DATA COLLECTION FREQUENCY AND MEASUREMENT PERIOD

STEP 5
Deciding How to Collect
the Required Data

So far, there are two other important issues that we have not paid much attention to—the frequency of measurement and the time period covered by the measurements. If you are a supplier of a physical good, then perhaps you would consider a measurement of delivery timelines. How often would you like to measure this performance indicator—every day, every week, every month? And how would you like this indicator presented to you— covering one day or a week, in continuous sequences of these short-span indicators, or as a constantly updated cumulative indicator covering the last week, month, or quarter? Our guess is that these are questions you might find difficult to answer just off the top of your head!

Let's try to define these two quantities more precisely and look into what impacts them:

- The measurement frequency indicates how often you make a new measurement. Typically, this is decided by two factors: measurement costs and the volatility of the performance dimension being measured. If the measurement in question must be performed manually—someone must either go out and collect the data or mine it from another source—then frequent measuring can be too cost- and time-consuming to be viable. In this case, you may have to settle for a lower measurement frequency, even if you would prefer to have the data updated more often. For data being collected automatically or at a very low cost, this is hardly an issue. On the other hand, determining the frequency for updating data is mostly a matter of how often and how much performance varies over time. For delivery performance in a business where delivery times change from hour to hour, you might want to measure on an hourly basis. If the performance measurement is absenteeism due to injury and the organization experiences 10 injuries a year, it is probably sufficient to measure this quarterly.

Definition of measurement frequency

- The time period covered by the measurements tells you how much data are included in the indicator presented. It can be a snapshot measurement of customer satisfaction with the service personnel in a store between 10 and 11 AM (time period of one hour), or it can be measured as the average customer satisfaction during the last month (time period of one month). In general, the time period should not be shorter than the time elapsed between when each measurement is taken, as this gives you only a random sample of the performance data. Even if the time period is longer than the time between measurements, but is still very short, you may find that any

Definition of measurement period

*Four combinations
of measurement
frequency and period*

attempt to track the trend and use it as an early warning system is impossible, since it will constantly fluctuate. Conversely, if you decide upon extremely long periods, then a trend actually present in the data material might be obscured and hard to detect because smaller deviations will have very little impact on the average value.

To provide more specific advice about this rather difficult decision, the following are four typical combinations and their preferred usage:

1. High measurement frequency, short measurement period: This combination is usually preferred for performance indicators whose main application are in the daily running of the process being measured, as it allows you to stay on top of development and take action quickly when required. However, such measurements will normally make it difficult to see any trends in the performance development. If each measurement is cumbersome or expensive to execute, this can be a rather costly approach.

2. High measurement frequency, long measurement period: This combination is best suited for rapidly changing data, where the main purpose is to use the measurements for longer-term improvement efforts. The longer measurement period makes it easier to spot development trends.

3. Low measurement frequency, short measurement period: As previously mentioned, a measurement period shorter than the time interval between measurements is generally not desired, as it will only give you a snapshot of less value than one of the other combinations.

4. Low measurement frequency, long measurement period: This combination is normally used for data that do not change very rapidly. The typical purpose is to use the measurements as input to improvement processes, especially since trend developments will appear quite clearly as long as the time period is not too long.

Since it can be difficult to predict how various decisions regarding frequency and time period will affect the usefulness of the performance indicators, the most appropriate way to determine these factors is often the proven approach of trial-and-error. It is naive to assume that you can decide your system once and for all and have it perform the way you want it to. Make a "best guess" based on the knowledge you have about your business and the performance measurement in question, see how it works, and change it if you are not satisfied with the outcome.

*Performance data
exhibiting seasonal
variation*

A final issue related to measurement frequency and time periods is seasonal changes. Quite a few performance indicators will display regular and quite predictable changes throughout the year, for example, the seasonal sales offerings for ski equipment, mosquito repellent, lawn mowers, and so on. If you try to continuously track a trend without being aware of such patterns, you risk seeing trends where there are only to-be-expected seasonal fluctuations. To handle such performance indicators, you must know that they do exhibit such fluctuations and the trend monitoring must be handled somewhat differently. Instead of following the continuous development in the indicator, a series of measurements for the same season must be used as the basis for trend analysis. For example, successive measurements for lawn mowers each spring could be used to watch for any trends, as well as a series for summer, fall, and winter measurements.

STEP 5
Deciding How to Collect the Required Data

9.5 DATA COLLECTION RESPONSIBILITY, DATA STORAGE, AND DATA SECURITY

Responsibility for collecting the performance data required by the system is another issue to be settled in this step of the design process. If you end up with an electronic system that automatically collects the performance data, then this is not an issue. However, you might want to assign the responsibility for ensuring that this automatic mechanism works and for taking action in case of problems or the need for maintenance of the system. For performance data that have to be collected manually, whether as input for an electronic or manual performance measurement system, there can be no doubts about the responsibilities and procedures for data collection. We have seen our share of situations where it is assumed that someone is collecting a certain piece of data but nothing has been formalized—this routine will of course break down at some point.

In systems where data are collected automatically, the issue of data collection responsibility is not so important

Fortunately, insuring yourself against these mundane problems is not difficult, it is simply a matter of going through all the performance indicators and checking that all required manual data collection has been assigned. This is one of the more rewarding tasks of the performance measurement system design team, since it is fairly straightforward and many people are eager to aid in the data collection, as it gives them first-hand access to the data. The main principle for appointing this responsibility is that the process owner—if the concept has been introduced to the organization, otherwise, the person in charge of the business process or area in question—must be responsible for collecting the required performance data from the process. This person might then delegate the task to people below him or her, but the main responsibility resides with this person.

Process owners or similar persons should be responsible for performance data from their processes or areas

After the data have been collected—electronically, automatically, or manually—they must be stored somewhere. As we have already mentioned, it is difficult to imagine a performance measurement system where the data are not stored electronically one way or another, so we will take this for

Storing of performance data

STEP 5
Deciding How to Collect
the Required Data

Data storage security

granted. The real question is: Which software should be used for storage? There are a multitude of different possibilities available, from simply storing the data in a spreadsheet file to the most elaborate database. Going into any detail about database design and management is truly beyond our scope of expertise, and again we feel confident that the IT-competent people of your organization can offer you assistance where needed. From projects we have been involved in, we have learned that some careful thinking about your storage, search, and data importing and exporting needs—both now and in the future—is time well invested. A logical structure of the performance data saves much time when trying to access the data later on, defining new performance indicators, retrieving pieces of data collected in connection with a different dimension of performance, and so on.

An essential consideration when discussing data storage is the security of the performance data. Remember that these are the key data describing the performance of your organization and its business processes in detail. Led astray, they would show the entire world—including your competitors—how well, or not so well, you do in a number of areas. Even if you do not permit these data to get lost or be made public, you might find yourself the victim of unlawful access attempts. Other threats are computer virus attacks or hackers attempting to erase or steal your performance data. Thus, however you decide to store the performance data, ensuring that there are security barriers keeping them off-limits to unauthorized people—internally and externally—is a chief issue at this stage. Again, it is beyond the scope of this book to delve into technical solutions, but there are many commercially available ways to protect data, from safes for paper, to firewalls, to encryption software for electronic databases.

9.6 DECIDING ON THE DATA COLLECTION APPROACH IN PBI, I³M

After having arrived at a set of performance indicators for the 22 business processes in the previous step, the performance measurement system design team realized that they were now at a crossroads. So far, they had not really touched upon the question of what the new system would look like. Once discussion began regarding whether to go for a full-fledged computerized system or stick with the semi-paper-based version they had before, there was almost no stopping it. In fact, at this point, the project was delayed by several weeks due to a deadlock.

The design team was less than enthusiastic about seeing all their work thus far materialize as a paper-based management reporting system, especially since the assessment of the existing system had revealed that this aspect did not work very well. Likewise, they were unwilling to approve a major project budget increase to buy or create an advanced computer solution. Thus, a lot of time was spent scanning the market for existing system offerings, culminating with the conclusion that they were all too costly. More time was spent discussing the possibility of producing an in-house solution with the internal service developers. A brief feasibility study was completed by a small three-man team of some of the most energetic whiz-kids in the development department, and the conclusion was that a system programmed in Java that would run on the organization's intranet could be produced within an acceptable budget.

Discussion continued until they finally decided to go for this solution. A small programming team was added to the design team so they could work closely together on the requirements specifications and the subsequent programming of the system.

While they were making this decision, the design team also commissioned the groups that originally developed the performance indicators to review all of the indicators and determine if and how the required underlying performance data could be collected. For several indicators, they concluded that different IT systems already captured and stored the data, thus making them easy to collect. A small number of indicators were based on information that the groups could not figure out how to capture, for instance the amount of energy wasted by not turning off computers at the end of the workday. About 15 other indicators would require some kind of manual operation to supply the required data. Responsibilities for these indicators were assigned to people who seemed able to easily handle the job, and they were required to work with the programming team to determine specifics for entering the data into the system.

The groups examining the data availability of the various indicators were also instructed to define the measurement frequency and time period covered for all the indicators. Some initial explanation by the design team was required before everybody understood the difference between the concepts and the significance of poor choices, a lesson worth remembering. In the end (after some help from the design team), the groups emerged with a neat table containing the names, definitions, formulas (where required), data collection method, measurement frequency, and measurement period for each indicator. Even though a fairly large number of people had so far been involved in the design process in some way, the design team printed this table on posters and hung them on walls in central locations throughout the company in an effort to create an even better insight into the development process. A notice was included on the poster that encouraged everyone with suggestions for improvements or adjustments in the indicators to pass them along to the design team. Quite a few surfaced, and many of them were taken into account when proceeding.

STEP 5
Deciding How to Collect
the Required Data

As previously stated, this process is not as sequential as our treatment in this book might indicate. For example, when working on the data collection aspect of the computerized system, the design and programming teams also started to look ahead to the data presentation side of the system. For some time these issues were actually handled simultaneously, but we will discuss this in the next chapter.

Chapter 10

Step 6: Designing Reporting and Performance Data Presentation Formats

As mentioned in the previous chapter, Steps 4, 5, and 6 in the design process are closely linked, and it is impossible to view the issue of how the performance data will be presented without regarding the data collection and storage questions addressed in chapter 9. Thus, some of the topics we raise here will be made with reference to previous discussions.

The most prominent issues the performance measurement system design team should deal with at this stage of the development process are:

- How the performance data should be treated—on paper or electronically

- Whether presentation formats should be predefined or customizable according to the wishes of the users

- User access to the different types and areas of the performance data and their openness inside the organization

- Data presentation formats, keeping in mind factors like ergonomics and the danger of data overflow

- How and why performance data will be used, to ensure that the selected reporting and presentation formats support them

We will examine each of these in sequence.

10.1 PAPER OR SCREEN

We have already discussed whether a performance measurement system should be manual/paper-based or electronic/computer-based. While we

STEP 1
Understanding and Mapping Business Structures and Processes

STEP 2
Developing Business Performance Priorities

STEP 3
Understanding the Current Performance Measurement System

STEP 4
Developing Performance Indicators

STEP 5
Deciding How to Collect the Required Data

STEP 6
Designing Reporting and Performance Data Presentation Formats

STEP 7
Testing and Adjusting the Performance Measurement System

STEP 8
Implementing the Performance Measurement System

STEP 6
Designing Reporting
and Performance Data
Presentation Formats

*Types of
performance data
presentation formats*

have concluded that it is virtually inconceivable to run a performance measurement system based only on paper (without some amount of data storage on a computer), this is not as clear when it comes to the presentation of the performance data. It is quite possible to store data in a database or spreadsheet file and make printouts of the performance indicator reports when required. While there may be a continuous scale from one extreme to the other, some possible ways to organize your performance presentation include (from least to most technical):

- Generating reports on paper for the user of the performance indicators

- Generating reports and sending them to users via e-mail in a file format, for example, spreadsheet or text

- Allowing the users themselves to access the data—either raw or compiled from the organization's server—thus eliminating the intermediary step of report production

- Improving the user-friendliness of the previous approach, by installing a report filter between the user and the database that will guide the user in defining the presentation format he or she would like

- Creating a piece of performance measurement system software that both has the report filter functionality mentioned above and allows the user to access the software and performance data through a Web browser from anywhere with Internet access

The next wave of technological development on the computer side is, of course, the advancement of handheld computers and mobile phones that can access the Web and run office software applications. While we have not encountered any such applications as of mid-2001, it seems a safe bet that within a relatively short period of time the next generation of performance measurement systems will utilize these gadgets to collect and present performance data.

*Operations and
maintenance costs of
manual versus
electronic systems*

As for deciding how to collect the underlying performance data from the organization and its operations, the question is: How much time and how many resources are you willing to invest up-front in the measurement system compared with what it will take to keep it running? In general, the more manual a solution you implement, the less time and resources it will take to set up the system, but it will also require more resources to perform the manual data collection and generate reports. With a higher degree of computerization, you normally have lower operational expenses, increased user-friendliness, and better overall benefits from the system, but at a higher initial investment. This is also a matter of organization size—where a small outfit of a few people can live with a very manual system, probably nothing less than a dedicated Web-based performance measurement system will work for a large organization.

In our view, if you are serious about your state-of-the-art performance measurement system and want to make it powerful and durable, you should choose a computer-based system right from the start. If you structure your database well from the outset, then setting up some sort of a Web page that will allow your employees to gain access to the performance indicators is a minor task. There are even some commercial packages available that can be designed to fit your organization's needs and can help you get started quickly.

10.2 PREDEFINED OR CUSTOMIZABLE REPORTS

We recommend aiming for a computerized performance measurement system for many reasons. The topic of this section addresses one reason, namely whether the system should present the users with predefined, standard performance reports (which can contain tables with numbers, text, charts, other graphics, and so on) or whether the user should be allowed to specify, every time, which indicators to review and how they should be presented to him or her.

In a manual system, anything but very standardized reports will be impossible. If you have ever had the "pleasure" of flipping through a typical periodic management report in a company of some size, then you understand why this is the least preferred option! Since the reports are generated at certain intervals and it is impossible to know in advance what will be useful from time to time, the principle employed is usually "better too much than too little." Every possible piece of interesting information is crammed into the report, some of which can run 50–100 pages long. We assure you that these reports are not in line with our view of a powerful, state-of-the-art performance measurement system. They drown readers with too much information and are of little use unless the recipients learn to identify which few indicators to focus on. Even then, incredible amounts of time and money may be spent preparing information that nobody needs. In a computer-based system, this problem can (notice the use of the word "can") be avoided. Even with this type of system it is possible to kill people with too much information, however the incentive is not the same as when trying to include everything when a report is being generated.

Generally, the performance measurement system is more useful if freedom can be given to the user to occasionally define which and how performance indicators should be presented. This is also an argument for

Paper-based management reports are not state-of-the-art

STEP 6
Designing Reporting
and Performance Data
Presentation Formats

investing wisely up front in a proper piece of software to handle the user interface. Designed with care, such an interface allows users to tailor reports and queries to their needs at any given moment (perhaps within boundaries defined by user access rights, to be discussed shortly), but also to design standard reports to avoid a specific query over and over again.

In our experience, once the initial amazement regarding the possibilities that a state-of-the-art performance measurement system offers for looking into every little aspect of the organization fades away, most users settle with a small set of indicators that they will check regularly. Allowing users to define such standard "gages in their dashboard" is a very user-friendly solution, especially if they are allowed to adjust the gages if and when necessary.

10.3 USER ACCESS TO AND OPENNESS OF PERFORMANCE DATA

We have already mentioned securing the organization's performance data against external and unintended access. A related issue is granting access levels to employees. Ideally, every member of the organization should be able to see all the performance data amassed in the performance measurement system; however, this might not be practical for every piece of performance data.

Access rights are a matter of policy

When defining performance indicators for different areas and business processes of the organization, it is quite likely that some will include data that are either personally sensitive (although we generally advise against measuring performance at an individual person level), unsuitable for access by everybody, or simply of no interest to most people in the organization. As such, which access rights are granted becomes, to some extent, a matter of policy.

Strike a balance between openness and data security

On one hand, we encourage you to keep your performance measurement system as open as possible, as this contributes to a good climate in terms of feeding data into the system and viewing it as a positive element, rather than as a threatening weapon for management. On the other hand, you must limit the access given to data that in any way are sensitive or confidential, no matter how open a climate you want to create. Our advice is to strike a good balance, but with emphasis on openness.

The worst failures we have encountered when working with performance measurement systems have occurred when top management has initiated the development of the system and then put a lid on it after it was completed. This creates distrust in the purpose of performance measurement, and it conveys the message that either there is something to hide or that performance indicators will be put to some sinister or malicious use. A striking example of this comes from our own organization, where part of the completed performance measurement is an annual quality of work life survey. A few years ago, a department scored quite poorly in this survey, which all employees knew would happen because they all had quite a few things to complain about, especially regarding management's handling of quality of work life matters. The report was compiled by a central safety, health, and environment office and returned to the department management team for discussion within the department, so they could take actions to improve the negative results. However, the report never left the management team and was not made public until somebody created quite a lot of noise demanding to see it. Naturally, there was not much enthusiasm for answering the survey the following year! Learn from this example and try to be as open as possible about the performance indicators your system can produce, unless there is a strong reason for keeping some under tighter control.

If you install a manual performance measurement system that requires somebody to compile the performance data, make reports (either on paper or a computer file), and send them to the users, then controlling which performance indicators various recipients have access to is, of course, no problem. It requires an extra link in the system, but enables you to control the flow of performance data easily.

In a computer-based system, where the users access the data directly and decide right then which performance indicators to review, access rights must be handled by the user administration layer of your system. We are currently involved in a project where a Web-based performance measurement system is being developed, and the access issue was solved quite nicely by programming a log-in session at the entry to the performance measurement system. Each user types his or her name and password and the system grants them access rights to the performance indicators they are allowed to see. At this log-in session, the users can go to their own previously designed profiles, thereby avoiding the need to set up their typical queries every time. This way, the administrator of the performance measurement system can precisely define and alter the user rights to the performance indicator database, from having everything available to every user to tailoring the access rights so that a typical user only sees the indicators for the process or processes he or she is involved in.

There are numerous ways to manage user access rights in your performance measurement system; this was merely an example. The key is to make it simple and strive for data openness unless there are very good reasons not to.

STEP 6
Designing Reporting
and Performance Data
Presentation Formats

10.4 INSTRUMENT PANEL DESIGN

Instrument panel design, like most issues we have discussed in these last two chapters, is also somewhat dependent on how you decide to implement your system—based on paper reports or on-screen displays, predefined reporting formats or customizable by the user. Both paper and a computer screen have their pros and cons in terms of displaying performance data, and, typically, what works well on paper might not on the screen and vice-versa. If you define the appearance of the performance indicator presentation beforehand, it is easier to ensure that the format abides by the most basic rules for making it clear and readable to the user. Controlling this is much more difficult if you allow the users themselves to set up their own screen layouts (just think of the basic color settings of any computer in your organization—they are originally based on a clean, light screen background and dark text, but we are confident that quite a few people have changed these settings to something much more elaborate, but a lot less readable).

Advice for instrument panel design

We consider the following to be basic rules for designing your instrument panel, independent of what medium will be used for presentation:

• The human mind is, in general, only capable of observing and digesting seven visual elements at one time. This means you should limit the instrument panel to displaying seven "gages" per sheet or screen. Filling the screen with 25 pie charts will only drown your users in information, rather than help them become better informed about the performance status of the business process in question. The order of design choices should be: What business process or area of the organization do I need to know the performance of? Which performance indicators will tell me this? How should I best picture them on the screen or paper to understand these indicators? One should avoid the approach of: What is this system able to deliver performance data about? How many performance indicators can we squeeze out of it? How can we put as many of them on the same screen or sheet of paper as possible?

• Human perception is also designed to focus clearly on a central focal area, and put less emphasis on visual elements peripheral to this area. It is therefore a good design principle to clearly show the user where the focal area is by clustering three to four of the most vital performance indicators there. If you need to include more in the same "picture," then scatter them away from this area.

• A "picture" is usually much easier to comprehend quickly than text-based information—words, sentences, or numbers in a table. In this context, a picture can be any type of a chart, graph, or color symbol, for example, a traffic light analogy, a gage or meter, or some other type of graphical display.

STEP 6
Designing Reporting and Performance Data Presentation Formats

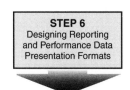

• Modern software—spreadsheets—allow you to depict numerical data in an almost unbelievable number of different chart types, and each chart type can come with or without shadow effects, in 2-D or 3-D appearance, with or without color, with or without labels, and so on. We advise you not to go overboard with all these possibilities. While it might sound old-fashioned, it is usually a good idea to stick to fairly simple chart types, without too much fancy "makeup," as most of these tend to take the users' focus away from the core information—the performance indicators.

• There is a reason why instrument panels that require the user to quickly interpret information and act on it, for example, in cars, airplanes, trains, and so on, all stick to the proven design of round gages, color-based warning lights, and perhaps audio alarms. As much as possible, you should try to stay with the same instruments, thus benefiting from close to 100 years of research that have gone into the design of instrument panels.

• One type of visual presentation not used in any of these vehicle types, simply because such data is rarely of interest to a driver, is trend charts. In your state-of-the-art performance measurement system, trend development of your performance indicators may very well be the most important information you can convey to the users, so this is an exception to the rule of striving for a vehicle-like instrument panel.

Our idea of one possible instrument panel design

We know it isn't the world's greatest performance measurement system instrument panel, but the example shown Figure 10.1 is meant to illustrate one possible design solution. It contains some old-fashioned gages, a trend chart, and a few green/yellow/red indicators. There are few visual elements, and the trend chart forms a natural focal area, with two peripheral areas—gages and color indicators. The circular shape is mere coincidence; but we hope this can give you an idea of how you can design your own instrument panel.

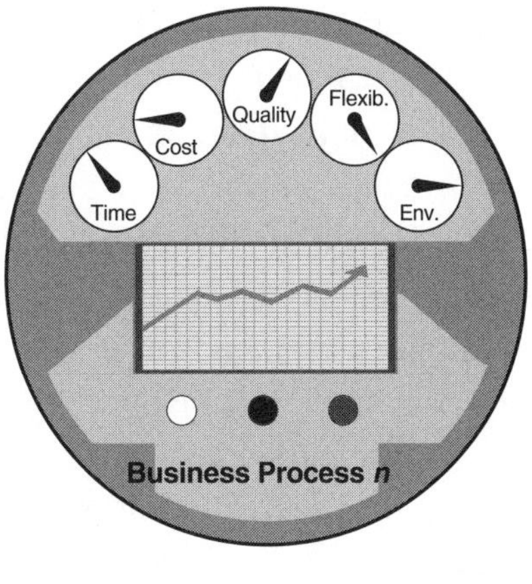

Figure 10.1 Sample instrument panel.

Design instrument panels for your business processes

The user interface can be based on the common click-and-call style of Web pages

As we have tried to indicate in our instrument panel, the indicators are related to one particular business process. If you remember the first few chapters and the measurement-based management model of Figure 3.1, we attempted to draw a picture of how there are connections all the way from the organization's vision and strategy down to its business processes. Our argument was that if you develop your business processes to reflect the requirements of your vision, strategy, and the requirements of your stakeholders, then your processes will be tools to implement the strategy and satisfy the stakeholders. Thus, if you measure the performance of these business processes, then you measure how well your tools work and, indirectly, how well you can implement your strategy and provide stakeholder satisfaction. This is why your state-of-the-art performance measurement system should focus mainly on your business processes.

Ideally, the users of the system should be able to access one or more performance indicators for each business process that they would like to examine. Whether one or several business processes are simultaneously displayed on the screen or in the report is more or less a matter of whether it will be too cluttered and you risk information overload. The main gate into performance indicators should, in our opinion, be the business processes. It is also quite possible that you need a set of process-independent performance indicators covering the entire organization or parts of it, for example, financial performance or safety and health data.

One way of structuring "gateways" into the performance database is a "point-and-click" system based on a logical hierarchical structure of the performance indicators, as shown in Figure 10.2. From this opening picture, the user can select a group of enterprisewide performance indicators (PIs) and be transferred to a screen where these are listed for further selection. Or the user can click a business process, chose among the applicable indicators, and even be allowed to click further to see the background data that indicator is composed of to better understand its levels and trends. Other options that can be added to this point-and-click system are the presentation format desired for the various indicators, which time periods they should cover, how coefficients relate to other indicators, and so on. This way, the performance measurement system takes on the look and feel of any Web page, where you click on links to proceed to other areas of the page structure. The advantage is that most people feel at home in such an environment, and you avoid having to type in complex commands or do some other type of magic to access the performance data you would like to see at any given time.

Again, your own imagination is the only real limitation in the design of the user interface side of your state-of-the-art performance measurement system. You can design it to be very comprehensive, with a tasteful screen layout and fancy graphics, or you can go for a rougher version, in the form

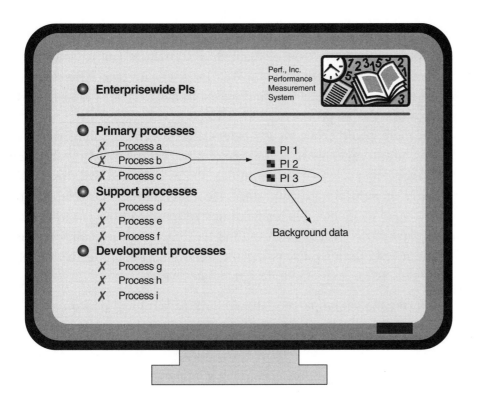

Figure 10.2   Performance data structure.

of paper reports or simple spreadsheet files distributed via e-mail. The key is to think through your needs at the outset and opt for a level that you think will be useful for some time, not something you must change within a few weeks because it is too cumbersome or complex. If possible, try to build in flexibility so that you can develop the system as the organization develops it expectations and needs for performance data.

Built-in flexibility

You should also keep in mind what we have already mentioned a few times: your first try at the system will rarely turn out to be perfect. It is a first draft, and the next step—the testing of this first draft—is bound to identify things you will have to change. It is better to arrive at something that is suitable for such testing and improve upon it, rather than spending forever trying to create the perfect solution on the very first attempt!

10.5 DEVELOPING THE PERFORMANCE DATA PRESENTATION FORMAT IN PBI, I³M

As stated at the end of the PBI, I³M section in the last chapter, the design team finally decided to go ahead with an electronic performance measurement system programmed by in-house resources. A main design decision

STEP 6
Designing Reporting
and Performance Data
Presentation Formats

was that the system should run on the company's intranet, allowing those responsible for the collection of manual performance data to enter these data from their own computer via a Web browser interface. This decision involved major implications for the discussions and decisions to be made in this step of the design process.

Since there would be a core computer-based system for facilitating data collection and storage, the only logical solution was to create a Web-based performance data access structure. Initial studies indicated that this would be a fairly straightforward job, since the programming knowledge and resources were available. The original design team and the programming team worked closely together to outline the functionality of this system, including a few sessions discussing the topic with people in the various business processes. Some main design choices were:

- In principle, all employees should have access to all performance indicators available in the system, unless there are specific reasons why some should be restricted.

- When connecting to the system via a Web browser, the users should type a user name and password.

- This log-on function should, in turn, invoke a predefined profile, specified by the user, that consists of the most used performance indicators and in the preferred presentation format. If a user decides to change these settings, a simple process should guide her or him through altering them.

- There should be a limit on how much data and how many indicators the users can cram onto the same screen, to avoid data blindness and overload.

- Based on some experimentation with formats and chart types, the system should limit the reporting formats to a few sound methods.

- As much as possible, the system should be based on a point-and-click interface, where users can click on an indicator to see the underlying performance data, click on these data to see their trends, and so on.

The actual programming of this system, up to the first prototype version, took about 10 weeks. At that stage, the system was made available to a few selected test users, who were asked to play around with and return impressions of the functionality, look, and feel of the user interface. These test users uncovered quite a few true bugs, some missing functionality, and had many—often conflicting—views on the appearance of the system. It took the programming team close to 10 more weeks to respond to the comments that were taken into consideration, but late one Friday afternoon the programming team manager declared version 1.0 complete.

We should point out that during the design process, the nature of the work saw a significant change at some point between Steps 4 and 5. Up to the point where the performance indicators had been designed, the project had seemed very much like an organizational development or strategy implementation project, dealing with softer management issues like strategy, business processes, employee involvement, and so on. From Step 5 and onward, the project took on much more of an IT system development nature, where the original design team became less active and the programming team took over the project to some extent. This was not due to the programmers' desire to "conquer" the project, but rather a result of the type of work involved, where much of the actual development of the system had to be done through programming. At times, the design team felt quite frustrated with how much time and effort it took to get the programmers to understand what they wanted the system to look like, and there were definitely some tensions between these two groups. But the job was eventually completed, and the design team was happy with the first version of the system ready for launch, even if there were still quite a few elements of the requirements specifications that had not been fulfilled. Perhaps their main concern was that no system manual had, as of yet, been produced due to the fast tracking of the programming aspect and the constant struggle for programming resources against projects developing new services for customers. This became a challenge in the test phase, which you can read more about at the end of the next chapter.

Chapter 11

Step 7: Testing and Adjusting the Performance Measurement System

STEP 1
Understanding and Mapping Business Structures and Processes

STEP 2
Developing Business Performance Priorities

STEP 3
Understanding the Current Performance Measurement System

STEP 4
Developing Performance Indicators

STEP 5
Deciding How to Collect the Required Data

STEP 6
Designing Reporting and Performance Data Presentation Formats

STEP 7
Testing and Adjusting the Performance Measurement System

STEP 8
Implementing the Performance Measurement System

First of all, let's be perfectly clear that this should not be the first time during the development process that your system is tested. If the development team arrives at this stage of the process with butterflies fluttering around in their stomachs, waiting for the first unveiling of the system, then you have gone about this process a little awkwardly. Naturally, you will need to check with the people around you—the future users of the system—to see how they like various design choices that were made at different stages in the development process. Moreover, if you are developing a computerized system, you will definitely have to test prototypes of different modules throughout the development. In this step, we refer to the first, more comprehensive testing of the entire system, where it is launched and "let loose" on the whole organization.

Even though the development team should have performed sufficient small-scale testing of the technical modules of the system to know that any major bugs or even system failures have been worked out, this is an exciting stage of the process. After having lived and breathed the performance measurement system for some time, watching it develop from scratch and into a prototype, the time has arrived when the rest of the organization will pass judgment on the efforts invested. Since there are probably as many different views on how the system should ultimately work and look as there are people in the organization, be prepared for negative feedback, especially since it is human nature to take for granted what we like and focus instead on things that should be improved. Do not be disappointed if the people around you don't seem to appreciate all the hard work you have put into the system; be pleased that they care enough about the performance measurement system to engage in the testing and provide feedback.

STEP 7
Testing and Adjusting
the Performance
Measurement System

*Issues that
should be tested*

11.1 ISSUES FOR TESTING

In this testing phase, there are really just a few major areas you need to focus on:

1. Does the performance measurement system cover the linkages from vision, strategy, and stakeholder expectations down to the business process level and the corresponding performance indicators? This relates to the overall design of the system and how well you have managed to place the system into a context that enables its use as a mechanism for alignment of the organization's resources toward a shared goal.

2. Does the performance measurement system measure what the organization actually wants it to measure? This addresses the quality that the performance indicator development job does and whether the validity of the indicators is suitable. For this test, it is necessary to take spot tests to ensure that the system is able to capture when the performance of a certain process changes.

3. Do the data collection mechanisms of the performance measurement system work as intended? This checks the input side of the system, that is, that established mechanisms and procedures for collecting performance data do, in fact, function and populate the performance database with the required information.

4. Do the performance data presentation modules of the performance measurement system work? This is the output side of the system, and the objective is to test whether the performance indicators are displayed properly and if the different users are able to gain access to their intended data.

5. Does the performance measurement system seem functional, so that employees will use it? Whereas the above issues have all been related to the mechanics of the system—that it works without bugs or malfunctions—this is more about subjective perceptions, which, indeed, need to be evaluated as well.

6. Does the performance measurement system seem capable of supporting the various functions needed by the users? Does it support improvement projects aimed at different business processes? Does it function as a daily decision-making support system? Can it be used in conjunction with incentive mechanisms? These are the last important issues to test, beyond the degree to which the users feel at home with the performance measurement system.

In our experience, these are the six main test questions to be asked. You can probably think of more. In every performance measurement system development process, there are singularities that the development team will feel the need to examine during the test phase, and these should, of course, be included during the testing.

11.2 EXECUTING THE TESTING

When beginning the test phase, we recommend that the development team put together a test plan to be distributed and communicated to all parties in the organization who will be affected by or will have to contribute to the testing. We have previously advocated a combined top-down/bottom-up development approach, where, to some extent, large portions of the organization become involved in the development work. However, during the development process, the level of involvement in general can vary considerably, both over time and among various people. In the test phase, many people will see the results of the development efforts for the first time, and many of them will have to play important roles in the testing if you hope to be able to carry out an extensive prototype test. It is therefore of vital importance that some type of structured plan is developed and relayed to everyone with a role to play in that plan.

Develop a test plan

The duration and extent of the test phase will naturally depend on the complexity and extent of the measurement system you have developed. It also depends on how thoroughly you want to try it out and how much you can comfortably leave to the first months of the operational phase following implementation. Normally, aiming to test every minute detail of the system before it is put to use constitutes overkill. There is no way you will be able to undertake a real-life testing of all aspects of the system, so you should focus on the main parts and accept that the time immediately after the system has been implemented must be considered as some kind of an extended test and streamlining phase.

So how do you actually go about testing these six main questions? Although there is no singular, correct approach to system testing, the following is an attempt at outlining some proven ways to proceed.

There are really only two ways to check how well the system reflects the overall structure of the business and manages to work as a mechanism for alignment of the organization's resources toward the goals of strategy implementation and stakeholder satisfaction. The first way is to use the system for a long enough period of time that it is possible to see these effects starting to manifest themselves. This will take much more time than we recommend you spend on testing the system; even if you did extend the

Testing the performance measurement system's ability for strategy implementation

*Testing the quality
of the performance
indicators*

test phase sufficiently for this to happen, you could never be sure whether it was the performance measurement system that contributed to these effects or something else. The second way is to choose a small group of knowledgeable people from different areas of the organization to perform a review of the system regarding these issues. Usually a map is drawn on a flip chart to assess how well the silver threads that link strategy to performance indicators stand out and prove that the system is capable of supporting the strategy. This definitely is not a precise test, but it is acceptable, and bringing in a few pairs of fresh eyes to review this issue can identify some areas for improvement.

To determine the suitability of the performance indicators, two tests should be performed. The first is a structured run-through of the different business processes and other possible areas of the organization deemed important to measure, to check that performance indicators have, indeed, been developed to cover them. This is a task that the performance measurement system development team can do more or less on its own, possibly with some input from other people. The second test is more complicated and is aimed at determining whether the defined performance indicators are actually capable of monitoring and detecting changes in the performance of the measurement objects. If there is an old measurement system still functioning in parallel with the newly developed one, it can be used to cross-check those performance indicators occurring in both systems. For all other indicators, the only way to perform such a test is by manually controlling the measurement results. This can be done in several ways:

- Manually collect the same data from the measurement system's performance data and the compilation of performance indicators for a process, calculate the same indicators by hand, and see if they match

- Feed the system artificial test data to simulate some performance indicators and see whether it returns the correct results

- Try to induce changes in the performance level of a business process (if it will not affect the true performance of the company significantly), either positively or negatively, and see if the performance measurement system is able to detect the changes

Given the varying nature of a complete set of performance indicators, you may have to try all of these suggestions if you want to test every indicator. Whether you should have such high ambitions at this stage is a matter of some debate, and you should use sound judgment when deciding that question. If the number of indicators is reasonable, try to run through them all; if it is very high, leave some of them for testing in the operational phase.

The same holds true for testing the data collection mechanisms of the system. It is perfectly possible to run through all the performance indicators and check whether the system has been able to retrieve the required data or if they turn up blank. If you settle for sample testing and the indicators turn out to be mostly working, it is usually acceptable to leave it at that and allow the users to discover any malfunctioning data collection routines later on. To check these, do some test runs with real-life data to see if the system, whether manual or automatic, is able to collect the data it needs to compile the performance indicators. To some extent, any problems here will be discovered when testing the performance indicators, as an empty indicator most likely signifies that there is a data retrieval error. If you only did sample testing of the indicators, this is a good exercise to check if and how well data are collected from various sources. Failure to retrieve pieces of data is a valuable finding, as is discovering if some of the data collection mechanisms are cumbersome, take too long to produce the data, or are expensive to run.

Testing the data collection mechanisms

To test the output side of the system, a useful approach is to establish a small, but varied, group to play around with the system for a few days to see if they feel comfortable with it. Such testing usually provides the most insight to the design team if it prepares a small questionnaire beforehand, either in the form of an evaluation sheet regarding different aspects of the system or a set of open-ended questions. As the test users experiment with the system, they keep this questionnaire close at hand and jot down their impressions and suggestions for improvement.

Testing the data presentation mechanisms

This test group can also be used to assess to what degree the system will actually be used once it is put into normal operation. Obviously you will not know the answer to this question until the system has been operational for a while, but you can get some idea by asking, on the test questionnaire, if people think they will use the system in the future based on their preliminary trial.

Testing the likelihood of future use of the system

In a computerized system, it is also worthwhile to install a simple feature to record the organization's usage of the system, either as a crude measure of how much total time the organization has been logged on to the system, or as a more detailed overview of the usage by different departments, organizational layers, or even individuals. Some time after going live, especially with the latter level of detail, methods can be initiated to inform slow users of the benefits of the system, target them for small training sessions in the use of the system, or ask them if they use the system so little because it is lacking something.

STEP 7
Testing and Adjusting
the Performance
Measurement System

Be cautious about changing the indicators—you might risk obscuring trends

The last important issue to test is how well the system is able to support the different purposes for which it has been designed. This is another aspect that can be difficult to test to any level of certainty during an intermediary test phase. So far, the best way we have seen is to make use of a small test population (either the same group as for the two last questions or a new one, to avoid stealing too much time from the same few people), and have them try out the system for a set of different tasks. By using a questionnaire or brief interviews, it is often possible to learn quite a lot—even from a limited number of test users.

However, even after all of these testing situations, we recommend that you keep the door open to any kind of feedback after the system is launched. Make it easy for people to reach the design team and offer reactions, suggestions for improvements, complaints, praise, or whatever feedback they might have. Demonstrate that good and realistic suggestions are taken into consideration, either by implementing them or explaining why they cannot be done. Remember, the system will never be finished—as with most other subsystems of your organization, it is a living, constantly evolving entity. Be aware, though, that implementing too many changes in a performance measurement system might make it less useful. If you are tampering with and constantly adjusting all the performance indicator definitions, then you might risk not being able to track trends, simply because you measure different processes in new ways all the time. Feel free to make whatever changes are necessary to the surrounding system, but be cautious about changing the indicators.

11.3 IMPLEMENTING CHANGES BASED ON THE TEST RESULTS

Implementing changes based on the test results is the obvious last step before the actual launch of the system. Unfortunately, it is a step quite a few design projects seem to forget or neglect to include in the planning of time or resource needs. It is often such a relief to reach the stage where there actually is a performance measurement system to test that it is perfectly normal to "block out" the thought of having to start over working on the system again and changing it. This is a big mistake!

We have yet to encounter a prototype performance measurement system that, while being tested, didn't uncover a number of issues—ranging from major design choices to minute details—that should ideally be changed. Even if the design team includes people from many different areas and layers of the organization, it always matures into a team that seems to influence each other into thinking similarly. As the development progresses, the entire team buys into the design choices they make and becomes blind to other possible solutions. Thus, when fresh minds are brought in to test the system, there are always suggestions for doing things differently.

That is not to say that you should take all of these suggestions into account, though. To many, it is a gut instinct to rebel against the existing, especially if they themselves had ambitions to be on the design team. After the testing has finished, or possibly during the test phase if different aspects are tested at separate times, the first important step is to take inventory of the change suggestions that have surfaced. These should be ranked in terms of:

STEP 7
Testing and Adjusting the Performance Measurement System

Ranking criteria for change proposals

- Soundness, that is, some evaluation of how good the idea is and how much it will improve the prototype system.

- Feasibility, an assessment of whether it is at all possible to change the system to adhere to the suggestion, or if previously made design choices render it impossible.

- Resource requirements, estimates of the time and money involved in making the change. If the two previous criteria prove that the idea is not worth much in terms of additional benefits to the system or is infeasible to answer to, then there is no point in spending time estimating the resource needs.

After the list has been compiled, and impractical suggestions excluded, the design team should carefully consider which changes it wants to implement. Remember that many of these suggestions have a nasty tendency of being interrelated—the moment you make one small adjustment, it can affect a number of the other suggestions or even create a need for new ones. For those changes chosen for implementation, it has often been wise to go ahead and have them implemented as quickly as possible, as both the design team as well as the rest of the organization are eager to see the end result.

The final outcome of this step of the design process should be an improved prototype version of your new, state-of-the-art performance measurement system. What remains is to launch the full-blown system into operation, which is the topic of the last step of the process.

11.4 TESTING THE PROTOTYPE PERFORMANCE MEASUREMENT SYSTEM IN PBI, I³M

We mentioned how the original design team had to play a secondary role in the development of the Web-based system compared with the programming resources. They should have taken advantage of this free time to plan the test phase and prepare a test plan for informing the organization about what

STEP 7
Testing and Adjusting
the Performance
Measurement System

was to come. Sadly, the design team became somewhat pacified with the programming team taking the lead role, and it did not function as well as it had during the first steps of the process. When the first system version was ready for its initial launch and testing, there had only been some preparatory discussions about how to approach this next step. This is a very important lesson to be learned from this case, since several weeks of progress were lost at this point. The summer vacation was only about a month away when the system was ready, and there would have been time for testing it during this period. However, since test plans were far from ready, the testing had to be postponed until after the vacation period.

The design team slowly regained momentum and spent the time left before the summer break preparing for the testing. To ensure that all issues to be tested would receive sufficient attention, they decided to split the testing into three tasks:

1. An assessment of the overall "measurement soundness" of the system, focusing on the system's ability to function in the larger context of the leadership and management of the organization, and to what extent the defined performance indicators seemed to measure the vital few aspects of performance, in order to avoid drowning the users in trivial performance data. A task force containing representatives from top management, a couple of staff functions, and a selection of business processes were commissioned to execute this assessment.

2. An in-depth testing of the functionality of the computer-based infrastructure, paying special attention to performance data security, data collection reliability, performance data quality assurance, user interface functionality, and the data presentation side of the system. For all of these issues, the main focus was on the system's ability to perform these functions properly and without malfunction, rather than the perceived user-friendliness or quality of the system (this was addressed in the last test task). Again, a small group—consisting of members from both the design and programming teams as well as a few volunteers from various areas and levels of the company—was assembled to complete this job.

3. Finally, a more subjective poll was taken of the future users' impressions of the new system, in terms of user-friendliness, the system's ability to support their daily work and improvement ambitions, the likelihood of the system being used and how much, and so on. The design team decided to fulfill this test task by setting up a few PC terminals around the company on which the system had been installed and inviting all employees to sit down and play with the system. When exiting the session, a simple survey was automatically launched on the screen, asking them to rate a number of aspects of the system.

We will not go into any detail about the test results here, as this was an extensive test that lasted about two months after summer vacations. All in all, the testing was successful, involving nearly 95 percent of the company's employees in one way or another. The amount of feedback was overwhelming, and much of it could not be handled right away. Many comments addressed similar aspects of the system but went in completely different directions, thus making it impossible to respond to them. Going one level above the nitty-gritty details of the test results, though, the general impression was that the users liked the system. Most felt that they had progressed decades from the old way of doing things and predicted that the system would be widely used and highly useful.

As the different sources of feedback started generating comments, the combined design/programming team gathered and structured them. Suggestions for changes were assigned to a change list, which was continuously reviewed to see which issues could be started on immediately and which should wait to see whether more pressing matters arose during the test phase. Again, we will not take you through the details of this, but many small and large changes were eventually made to the system—although far from everything that had been commented on. When version 2.0 of the system was ready for final implementation, the project had lasted close to a year. It is worth noticing that even though this exceeded the original plans by two to three months, there was very little grumbling in the organization, which we believe was a result of the extensive degree of involvement of a large number of people in the development and testing process.

STEP 7
Testing and Adjusting
the Performance
Measurement System

Chapter 12

Step 8: Implementing the Performance Measurement System

STEP 1
Understanding and
Mapping Business
Structures and Processes

STEP 2
Developing Business
Performance Priorities

STEP 3
Understanding the
Current Performance
Measurement System

STEP 4
Developing Performance
Indicators

STEP 5
Deciding How to Collect
the Required Data

STEP 6
Designing Reporting
and Performance Data
Presentation Formats

STEP 7
Testing and Adjusting
the Performance
Measurement System

STEP 8
Implementing the
Performance
Measurement System

The title of this chapter might give the impression that, so far, the design team has designed and built the measurement system in some remote, secret room, and now it is time to install this complete system in the organization. This is, of course, not how such development processes work.

If you followed our advice about employing a combined top-down/bottom-up approach, then the rest of the organization was informed about the efforts from the very start and throughout the entire design process, and various people from the organization have been involved in the project. There have been discussions at many levels and in many areas of the organization, and as the system has evolved, parts of it have gradually been installed in areas such as computer systems and inside processes. In the previous step, tests of the system were performed, and following a phase of adjustments based on the test results, the time has now come to formally put the system to use.

While this is not as dramatic a moment as the unveiling of an edifice, it is still usually a good idea to make it into some kind of a milestone. This represents the culmination, thus far, of a major undertaking by the organization—especially by the design team and those most closely involved in the design process—and it is a nice opportunity to crown their efforts with an official moment. Such a moment also lends itself to a more formal presentation of the system, as well as to kick off its use.

So what does this mysterious implementation phase entail? Some important activities, some of which might actually have been addressed in earlier phases of the design process, are:

STEP 8
Implementing the
Performance
Measurement System

- Physically installing the system and making it operational and accessible to the users.

- Developing and distributing information about the system, possibly including some kind of instruction manual.

Implementation phase tasks

- Announcing the official kick-off and formal launch of the new system.

- Providing necessary training in the use of the system to those people in the organization who will use it.

- Allocating necessary resources to answer questions about the system after it has been launched, stand-by to correct any malfunctioning, and generally evaluate the system after it is first put to full-blown use.

12.1 INSTALLING AND LAUNCHING THE PERFORMANCE MEASUREMENT SYSTEM

Launch = setting the data collection mechanisms in motion

As mentioned in the introduction, parts of the system have been gradually implemented during its development and testing. This can sometimes involve nothing more than providing links from the users' terminals to the new system. If you are implementing a more manual system, it is often a matter of making data collection forms available and instructing people where to deliver their reports. In both types of systems—computerized and manual—the most visible action is to "push the button" for the data collection procedures. Once the underlying performance data start to come in and populate the system database, performance indicators gradually become available to the users and the system is up and running.

Try to time the launch to the start of dominating measurement periods

One thing to consider when planning this moment is timing. If you remember the discussion about time periods covered by the different measurements in chapter 9, you will recall that many of the performance indicators will cover short time periods like weeks, days, or even hours. Some, on the other hand, will be measured for longer periods of time—months, quarters, perhaps even years. To get off to a good start, it is often wise to have the launch date for the system coincide with the starting date of a dominant measurement period. For example, if you know that many of your indicators will be measured on a quarterly basis, these indicators will be operational from the very first day if you launch the system on the first day of a quarter. If hitting a quarter start date is difficult, at least try for the first day of the month. In cases where you have to settle for a day in the middle of a period, you will either have to wait for indicators affected by this or try to feed the system old, previously available data.

When you actually do push the button and launch the system, obviously any manual operations required to run it will have to be described and delegated to people who will carry them out. It is not good to launch the system first and then start thinking about how to obtain the required data. Make sure that such tasks are covered by procedures explaining how and when to perform them, including necessary data collection forms, any measurement tools required to collect these data, and any other information believed to be important to ensure that the system is running smoothly.

During the last weeks before the launch date, it is usually wise to prepare the organization for the implementation of the new system by issuing periodic information about when it is to be launched, when people are supposed to start using it, where more information can be obtained, and so on. Try to build a level of expectation in the organization that will contribute to making the launch an important and anticipated event and ensure that people are aware of the benefits of the system when they start to use it. Please also keep in mind that it is vital to be honest about the system's abilities and, not in the least, its lack thereof. The most effective way of ensuring that the system will be a failure is to hoist the system onto a pedestal and proclaim the marvels it will work when you know it has its limitations. Try to be realistic in the prelaunch marketing of the system, and focus on the aspects you know will be appreciated.

As the launch date approaches be assured that along with any expectations, some level of anxiety is also building up in the organization. If performance measurement has not been practiced earlier, there are bound to be many people who feel unsure about how this will work—and how it will affect their existence at work. One way to counter this effect is to preemptively address some of their fears. We have seen a few excellent examples of how fear of and even hostility toward a coming performance measurement system have been reduced very effectively by producing leaflets or bulletins that answer some difficult questions related to the new system. Inspired by Kaydos' book *Operational Performance Measurement: Increasing Total Productivity* (1999) it is smart to address such issues as:

• Why do we need performance measures? The best answer is: it will help us know what we are good at and, even more importantly, what we are not so good at, so that we can improve and serve our customers better.

• How will the measures be used? To this question, it is vital that the answer emphasizes that the performance indicators will be employed to identify the performance of business processes, not the level of effort expended by individual employees. The indicators will mainly be used to identify business processes in need of improvement, and to measure whether improvement efforts produced the expected results.

STEP 8
Implementing the Performance Measurement System

Market the system before the launch

Issues about the performance measurement system that should be preemptively addressed

STEP 8
Implementing the
Performance
Measurement System

• Will the measurements be used to find faults and punish people? Assure the employees that no one will be reprimanded or fired for making mistakes. Rather, if the performance of a business process turns out to be less than expected, this knowledge will be used to improve the framework for doing a good job.

• What can I gain from this? First of all, the true answer is that the new performance measurement system will help the organization improve, become more solid, and provide more secure employment—possibly even be able to pay better wages. Further, it will allow each and every person to gain insight into how their work will advance the goals of the organization, thus making their work more rewarding.

• Will we be able to see the measures? Be honest about this question. If all or most of the performance database is going to be open to everyone, say so. If the general approach is that performance indicators for a business process will only be available to those working in that process, be clear about this and the fact that data from other processes will be concealed. If the intention is to allow only a select group of users to access the data (which rarely is a good idea), be honest about that too.

12.2 TRAINING IN THE USE OF THE SYSTEM

If you have decided on either a manual system, where reports are delivered directly to the users without their having to ask for them, or a system to which access is limited to a few selected members of top management, then training is probably not a big issue. In the latter case, you will need to provide the selected people with enough insight into the system to be able to use it, but the training is much less extensive than for an organizationwide, open system. In the former case, there is no need for training in the technical use of the system, as it consists of reading a paper-based report or opening a file to read it. However, there is probably still a need for training in the use of the performance indicators. Being able to gain access to them is only the first step; if the new performance measurement system is to provide the expected benefits to the organization, then the users should understand how to apply the performance indicators for whatever purposes necessary. This is something all users need to be trained in, no matter which type of system or how many users there are. We will discuss this in more detail shortly.

In the case of a computerized system that has a relatively large number of users throughout the organization, planning and executing the required training is an important task in the implementation phase (or for its preparations). Training for the new performance measurement system is very much different than training for any other system that is installed in the organization, so we will not try to provide you with any specific performance measurement system training guidelines here. Further, there is a vast library of books on the subject of organizational training. However, some general advice to keep in mind regarding the training task at hand is:

STEP 8
Implementing the
Performance
Measurement System

*General
training advice*

- The effectiveness of a training program's execution is directly proportional to its level of preparations. Thus, planning the rollout efficiently, preparing training material well in advance, preferably having the system instruction manuals or their likes available during the training, and so on, all contribute to a successful training and, subsequently, more competent use of the system.

- Training "on paper" can be a suitable introduction, but to teach the practical task of using a performance measurement system, the users need the opportunity to play around with the actual system during the training.

- If possible, have the design team do most of the training, as they know the contents of the system in great detail, as well as the purpose of the different parts and how they are supposed to work.

- Consider bringing someone with a teaching background into the preparations for and execution of the training.

A final word about training—please do not be intimidated by our advice regarding training material, instructional support, and so on. If you belong to a small or medium-sized organization, where it is fairly easy to identify and contact the targeted users of the system and/or the performance measurement system under implementation is fairly straightforward to use, then the training required can be very limited and quickly completed. In some cases, it might even be a matter of distributing instructions for the most frequently used applications.

12.3 POST-IMPLEMENTATION SUPPORT

The last issue we will deal with in the implementation step is what happens after you have "pushed the button" and the system is up and running. It would be naive to assume that implementation is complete when the system has physically been put into action, because the implementation step can

*Issues for
post-implementation
support*

drag out considerably before you can actually close it. Some considerations for this period of the process are:

• As system users start getting into and become more demanding in its use after their first fumbling attempts, they are bound to come up with a multitude of different questions, requests for changes, suggestions for improvements, and so on. To avoid the users feeling as if they and the system have been launched into a vacuum, it is important to provide resources and "an address" where these inquiries can be directed. This should be a combination of someone knowledgeable about the system at the functional level, someone who knows the technical parts of a computerized system, and someone who can record and file change suggestions.

• Change suggestions cannot just be filed and stored away—they must be exploited to improve the system. Thus, it is necessary to set up some kind of a structured procedure for gathering and reviewing these suggestions. At least part, if not all, of the system design team must normally be involved in this task, and it is important to separate the useful and valuable comments from those that can be ignored. You are certain to receive many suggestions reflecting very specific personal wishes of some individuals, and these must be at the absolute bottom of the prioritization list. Other suggestions will probably require such extensive changes in the system that they are impractical to deal with. Anyway, it is important to perform this type of winnowing to ensure that you proceed with feasible changes that will contribute to improvements in the system that will be appreciated by many of its users.

• As any changes—minor or major—are being made to the system, remember to inform all users about them, update instruction manuals, and, if necessary, provide additional training.

Finally, let us repeat that your new, state-of-the-art performance measurement system, if it remains "forever" in its existing form, will not remain state-of-the-art for very long. It is unavoidable that dynamic changes in the organization's surroundings, the organization itself, its vision and strategy, new knowledge about performance measurement, new technological opportunities, and so on, will make it necessary to perform "generation" updates of the system from time to time.

*Consider appointing a
system review board*

To ensure that such updates are completed, and also to avoid making incoherent, partial improvements to the system all the time, a good working solution we have observed is to appoint some kind of a system review board. This review board is responsible for undertaking periodic assessments of the system and to what extent it satisfies current conditions. Such assessments are often held annually, but there may be good reasons to have them either more or less often, depending on the organization and its environment. We also recommend that such a comprehensive assessment be made a while after the launch of the system, after it has had time to fall into step with the organization and get into regular use, so you can pick out any elements not working as intended that were not captured in the test phase. The same board should also screen the submitted improvement suggestions to perform this winnowing.

Placing the system in a larger picture is the last important topic about performance measurement systems we will cover. If you run through the system design process we have detailed, we feel confident that you will end up with a good and working performance measurement system. That is not enough to justify the investments in the system; it must be put to use, and used correctly, to achieve the initial objectives for its development—increased employee motivation from receiving continuous feedback, creating improvements, aligning the resources of the organization, and so on. How to achieve this, now that you have the system, is the topic of the next and final chapter.

12.4 IMPLEMENTING THE NEW STATE-OF-THE-ART PERFORMANCE MEASUREMENT SYSTEM IN PBI, I³M

We said at the beginning of this chapter that this final step of the design process should not be some kind of an official unveiling of a well-hidden secret. This was true at PBI, I³M, because so many people had been involved in the development and testing of the system. After completing the changes based on the test results, the design team quickly decided on a date when the system would be put to formal use. Before then, a few things had to fall into place:

• The programming team had to roll out the system throughout the organization—install it on the server, activate the data collection procedures, and insert the system link into the Web browsers of the users. User names and passwords were issued, and access rights for any restricted data were also determined.

• One of the people working on developing user guidelines for new services for PBI, I³M's customers was assigned to produce some simplified guidelines for the system. These were provided online and accessed through the same Web browser used to access the system, and consisted of flowcharts describing how to perform different functions in the system.

STEP 8
Implementing the
Performance
Measurement System

• For two weeks, sessions were arranged in the cafeteria between 7 and 10 PM to demonstrate the system and its functionality to the users. These were not mandatory, they were simply advertised, and every night pizza was served. The turnout was acceptable, and by the end of this training period, about 80 percent of the employees had attended one or more of these sessions.

On the launch day, the system was opened up to all users—and then froze half an hour later. During the next few days, the system went down several times, requiring massive efforts from the programming team to get it up and running after each breakdown. Some further modifications were made, and as the number of simultaneous online users gradually decreased (as the first curiosity passed), the system stabilized. Over the next weeks, several small and large problems popped up, making this period—which was supposed to be a time of glory and admiration—hard work as bugs were corrected here and there. In hindsight, the design and programming teams concluded that the testing had been too limited in terms of number of users—many problems occurred only when more than 50 users were accessing the system at the same time.

Close to 15 months after the project commenced, the design team formally dissolved after celebrating the implementation of the system. A smaller team of three people was assigned the responsibility of monitoring the use of the system and making any changes required to keep it functioning, and they decided to perform a larger evaluation one year down the road.

As this final chapter of the case is being written, the system has been operational for about eight months. Although some small bugs have a tendency to pop up occasionally in the system and there are quite a few requests for new or adjusted performance indicators, the overall impression is that the system works well. Most people use the system at least once per week, and the performance development trend is increasing for a large number of the business processes. If this book comes out in a revised version, we will provide an update of the situation!

Chapter 13

Using the Performance Measurement System

There are several possible applications of performance measurement throughout an organization (see chapter 2). In this chapter, we will focus on a few of these applications and discuss how the system can be exploited to attain certain objectives. These are the applications for which management and employees will typically use the system so it is important to provide these users with insight into how the system can be most effectively employed in this respect. There are probably other applications many will consider important to include in this set, but we have chosen to focus on the following few:

- To monitor performance levels and their development for business processes or other areas of the organization

- For decision support in the daily operational management of the organization

- To conduct diagnostic self-assessments of the organization

- To undertake a benchmarking study of the organization

- To facilitate process improvement work in the organization

Guidelines for five main performance measurement system applications

To some extent, with the progression through this list, the complexity of the applications increases. Thus, it is quite normal that during the first period after implementation, the system is employed for the simpler tasks at the top of the list. As confidence in and skills for using the system increase, users gradually go further. When they realize that the system can support all of these applications, this becomes a continuous circle where increased use produces increased benefits, and so on.

In the following discussion, we will present some rather simple flowcharts to illustrate how your new, state-of-the-art performance measurement system can be used to accomplish the tasks listed above. These flowcharts are accompanied by explanations and examples. Their main purpose is to inspire the performance measurement system design team to use the material to educate users of the new system in its use.

13.1 PERFORMANCE MONITORING

Performance monitoring—the most common usage of the measurement system

The first flowchart (Figure 13.1) covers using the performance measurement system for monitoring the performance levels of a business process. This is perhaps the most common usage of the system, where a process owner (if the concept has been introduced into the organization), a manager, an employee inside the process, or somebody else wants to monitor the performance level of a certain process. It is also used for the early warning capability depicted in Figure 2.2.

Let's imagine that a monitored business process is customer handling in a bank. The process owner (one has been appointed in this bank) consults the set of individual performance indicators for this process (notice that the step will be the same whether it is requesting a paper report from a central statistics department or bringing them up on her computer screen). First, she will typically check whether the individual performance indicators are within the predefined limits of performance, for example, waiting time in line, the number of errors occurring during customer handling, and so on. If not, the next logical step is to look into the root causes why they are not (some tools for conducting such an analysis are presented later in this chapter). If the investigation uncovers that some freak occurrence caused the deviation, for example, a once-a-decade power failure, she moves on.

If a more systematic error was the cause of the situation, one that could be expected to recur—for example, understaffing due to sickness—then the process should be put on a list of processes waiting to be dealt with in improvement projects. This is just a general way of saying that the process should be dealt with further, not that the bureaucracy of such a list is important. The process owner herself can initiate such an improvement project or she can leave it to a special improvement team who will handle it based on such a waiting list. With this outcome, performance monitoring has served its purpose: it has uncovered less than acceptable performance, and the job can be completed by generating some kind of a report on the findings. Although we have said nothing about the recipients of

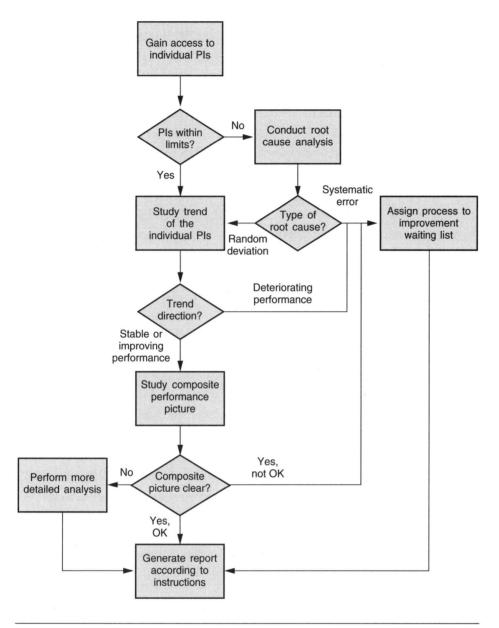

Figure 13.1   Business process performance monitoring.

such a report, it is often stored by the process owner and also sent to her superior or a centralized quality department.

If the individual performance indicators are within the limits, then trend is the next issue in the process. Again, we assume that the performance measurement system is capable of supplying such trend data, preferably in a graphical format, and the point is to determine whether the trend is

Control limits

deteriorating, remaining stable, or improving. If the time spent by the average customer waiting in line is slowly, but surely, rising the process is considered to be in need of improvement. If all trends seem in order, the last study is of a more overall, composite picture of the entire process's performance.

There are several ways to compose such an overall performance picture, but a fairly common one is to assign weight factors to all individual performance indicators, calculate the percentage target deviation for each, find the combined target value deviation factor for the entire process, and, based on this, assign a color code or some other score for the overall process. An example for the customer handling process is shown in Table 13.1.

Targets have been set for the three performance indicators in the example, with weight factors assigned totaling 100 percent. The actual performance is measured and the percentage deviation from the target calculated at 35 percent, 6 percent, and 40 percent. According to the performance standards required by the customer handling process, a deviation factor between 0 and 20 percent is considered OK (green), 20 to 40 percent should be monitored closely (yellow), and more than 40 percent is unacceptable (red). In the last column, these deviation percentages have been multiplied by the weight factors to produce weighted deviation factors, whose sum is 33.15 percent. The composite deviation factor is in the yellow zone, indicating the process is in jeopardy of going beyond the limits.

Having compiled this composite picture, the next step for the process owner is to assess whether this picture is clear or tells an ambiguous story. In this case, even if the overall score was yellow, it is clear that some heavily weighted performance indicators were in the yellow zone, which is not very encouraging. She would have to initiate a more detailed analysis of these performance indicators and discuss in the report she produces in the final step whether any actions are required. The other outcome from this

Table 13.1   Composite performance picture.

PI	Target	Weight Factor	Performance	Target Deviation	Weighted Target Deviation
Waiting time	2 min.	0.35	2.7 min.	35%	12.25%
Seating capacity	95%	0.15	89%	6%	0.9%
Clerical error frequency	1%	0.50	1.4%	40%	20.0%
		1.00	Weighted, total target deviation	33.15%	

assessment is that the composite picture is indeed clear and doesn't hide any surprises. It may be telling a clear negative story, in which case the process is again flagged for being in need of improvement, or a clear positive story, in which case this is reported and the job closed for now.

Of course, for this process of performance monitoring to be useful, it must be repeated at periodic intervals.

13.2 DECISION SUPPORT IN DAILY OPERATIONS

Decision support in daily operations is an application that lends itself very poorly to any generalization. There are literally thousands of different situations that might arise in your organization that would benefit from having suitable performance data available to offer insight and facts on which to base a decision. To make the flowchart in Figure 13.2 simple, we have made this a "question" that needs answering.

This application is difficult to generalize

To link this rather abstract task to something more specific, consider a customer's request of a manufacturing plant to deliver 100 units of a rather complex product within seven weeks. This is a typical example of a "question" that can pop up at any time and be supported by the performance measurement system. The first step is to determine if there are any relevant performance indicators in the system to support this decision. If yes, these must be examined.

A performance measurement system probably contains performance indicators for the delivery performance of the company. These can be used to calculate the average delivery time of similar orders in similar situations and thereby predict whether this particular order can be delivered within seven weeks. If the available performance data do indeed produce an answer, be it positive or negative, the procedure is finished. If not, or if there are no relevant performance indicators in the system to answer the question, one further step must be taken to figure out what performance data would enable answering the question.

If these data are in the performance measurement system, but in the form of underlying performance data that do not show up in the performance indicators, then they must be studied to see if they produce the answer. If not, the next question is whether these data can be produced in some way, either from other databases in the organization or by manually collecting the missing pieces. If so, these must also be examined. If not, the system is again unable to help out in this situation.

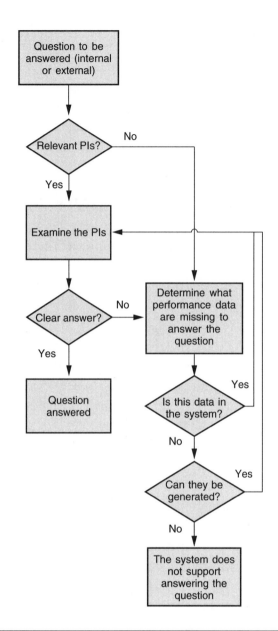

Figure 13.2 Decision support based on performance data.

13.3 CONDUCTING A DIAGNOSTIC
SELF-ASSESSMENT

The performance measurement system supports self-assessment

As explained earlier, self-assessment is a less frequent and more comprehensive diagnostic performance measurement than the more operational performance measurements we are primarily dealing with here. However, when conducting such a diagnostic self-assessment to determine the general shape of the different business processes and areas of the organization, the performance data collected by the performance measurement system are exceedingly helpful. Usually, none or much less data have to be collected during a self-assessment if a performance measurement system exists than if it does not. The flowchart in Figure 13.3 depicts the general steps when employing such performance data in a self-assessment.

The first step is to decide what business processes or areas of the organization should be covered by the diagnosis. There is no "rule" saying a self-assessment should encompass every part of the organization; very often different areas are covered at different frequencies. Of a set of 32 business processes in an organization, there might be a procedure for evaluating eight of these every quarter through a self-assessment. When the measurement objects have been established, identify suitable performance indicators for their diagnosis—preferably without too much regard for what is available in the performance measurement system. After these have been identified based on what indicators are best suited for the purpose, the next issue is whether these can be found in the system. If not, they must be collected manually. For instance, if one of the processes being diagnosed is a manufacturing process, and you really want to know how the operators feel about working conditions, you should not be discouraged from assessing this aspect just because there are no performance indicators covering it in the measurement system. Conduct a manual survey and combine the results with the other data that the system can provide information about.

When all required data have been gathered, the real job of the diagnosis is aggregating the separate indicators into more comprehensive ones and then analyzing them. Remember that the main purpose of a self-assessment is to gain a quick overview of large parts of the organization, mainly to reveal symptoms that something is not in the preferred state—much like your annual health checkup. You should look for areas with decreased performance compared with the last round of self-assessment, indications that things might start to slip, unusually high performance levels that might suggest that too many resources are applied to one area, and so on. At the end of this chapter, we will also present some analysis tools that can be applied at this stage.

Sometimes, though, the picture is not clear after this analysis. There might be many symptoms pointing in different directions, a few processes might seem to warrant a more in-depth examination, or a closer scrutiny of some areas may need to be conducted now and then. If so, a more dedicated analysis team should be established to undertake this scrutiny and

An approach to self-assessment

Self-assessment is really like an annual health check

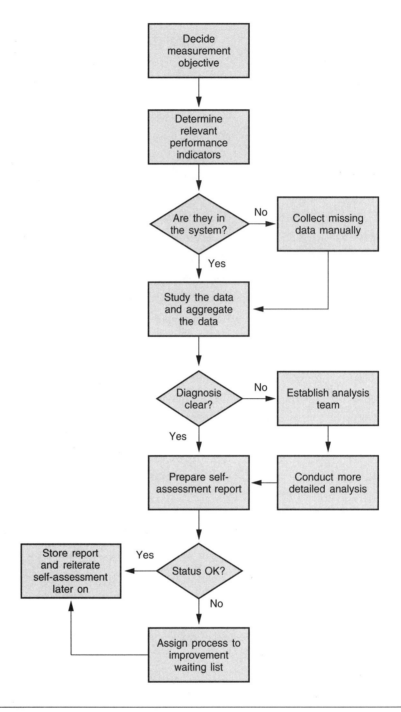

Figure 13.3 Diagnostic self-assessment using performance data from the performance measurement system.

report back in more detail. The outcome of the self-assessment should be a diagnosis report that can be filed together with previous reports for comparison at the next juncture. Any business processes or areas that need improvement are assigned to the previously mentioned prioritization list (which will be discussed further during the process improvement section following).

13.4 USING THE PERFORMANCE MEASUREMENT SYSTEM FOR BENCHMARKING PURPOSES

By continuously measuring the performance of different business processes over time and compiling trends of this data, you are able to monitor the performance development of these processes. There is, however, no external reference to tell you what level of performance you are achieving on a more global scale. This can be compared to stepping outside every morning to check the temperature without reading a thermometer, but rather by noticing whether it is hotter or cooler than yesterday. For an inaccurate impression of the temperature and whether to wear more or less clothing than the day before, this is fine. If you have a thermometer, you can put the temperature into context and such a reading will be even more valuable.

An isolated performance measurement lacks an internal reference

This applies to performance measurement as well. Unless you are able to determine an external reference point for your internal measurements, trend is really all you can hope to achieve. If you measure employee turnover and find that there is a decreasing trend from 15 percent down to 12 percent, then this is certainly a positive sign that the indicator is improving. However, the picture becomes dramatically different if your competitors average 7 percent. Performing a benchmarking analysis now and then to establish such external reference points is normally well-invested time and money. The flowchart in Figure 13.4 outlines the common steps in such a process.

Since benchmarking can be a resource-intensive project, especially if you do both performance and process benchmarking, it is impractical to cover all your business processes through benchmarking studies. Therefore, the first step is typically to decide which process—or small number of processes—to cover in the study. If you concentrate on the human resource management side, for example, it would be logical to include the most important processes in this area: recruiting, training, management of the quality of work life, and so on. Before you even approach any benchmarking partners, you should do your homework and gather all performance data from the performance measurement system about these processes.

Benchmarking is a resource-intensive undertaking

Searching for benchmarking partners can be a tricky task, but if you consult various sources—both internally and externally—for ideas, it is normally feasible to come up with three to five relevant benchmarking partners. Relevant implies that: they are not so different from your own organization that any comparison is bound to be off the mark; together, they represent some kind of an average, not merely extremes in either direction; and they are willing to enter into a benchmarking study with you. For example, for a process such as human resource management, which is usually

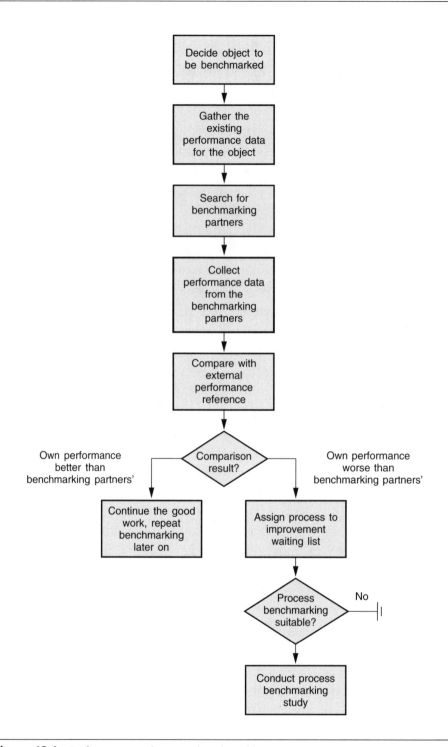

Figure 13.4 Performance and process benchmarking.

not distinctive from industry to industry, finding benchmarking partners in other industries can be a good idea, as this avoids your competitors' reluctance to share information. After identifying partners, you collect the equivalent performance data about their processes and use this data to judge your own performance level. In terms of performance measurement and value added to your internal measurements, this is the most important step.

Performance benchmarking

However, benchmarking has the potential for further added value. Once you determine that one or more of your benchmarking partners outperform you, there is no reason why you should not use this knowledge for improvement. By going deeper into a process benchmarking study, you can try to figure out what the benchmarking partner does that enables its superior performance. Based on this insight, you can probably achieve significant improvements in your own process. This is, of course dependent upon the benchmarking partner's willingness to let you study its processes in more detail. Surprisingly often, organizations are willing to enter into mutual exchanges of such information, but you must be prepared to allow the partner to study one of the processes where you excel. For a more detailed treatment of benchmarking, you can look up one of several excellent books by Robert Camp (1989, 1994, 1998) or *The Benchmarking Handbook— Step-by-Step Instructions* co-written by one of the authors of this book (Andersen and Pettersen, 1996).

Process benchmarking

Benchmarking is just one of several available tools for creating business process improvement. Business process improvement in general, based on the performance measurement system, is the last topic of this chapter.

13.5 BUSINESS PROCESS IMPROVEMENT SUPPORTED BY THE PERFORMANCE MEASUREMENT SYSTEM

Usually, the performance measurement system will help you decide which business processes display performance developments that require improvement efforts to be initiated (as shown by the previous flowcharts, where the result has often been that a process has been assigned to an improvement waiting list). The two other important functions of the measurement system are to provide insight into why a particular business process is performing poorer than expected, and allow follow-up measurements during and after an improvement project to determine whether it produced the desired improvements. The last flowchart we have included, Figure 13.5, illustrates its usage for these purposes.

Throughout the treatment of the other applications of the performance measurement system and its data, we have referred to an improvement prioritization waiting list. This list is merely a reflection of the fact that at any given time in any given organization, there will always be many business processes and their issues that you would ideally like to improve and

Improvement prioritization waiting list

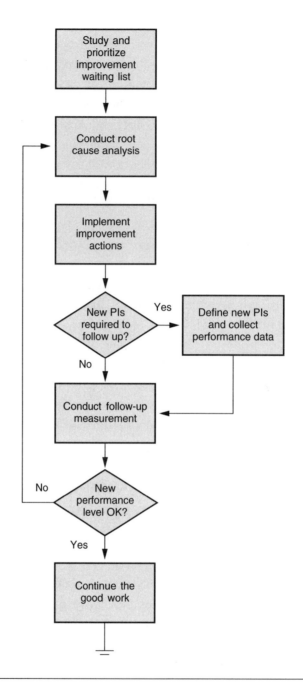

Figure 13.5 Using the performance measurement system for process improvement.

address in detailed analysis and improvement projects. Arguably, most organizations cannot afford the time or money required to attack all of these at the same time. Thus, these improvement needs must be addressed in a systematic manner to avoid the anarchy that can arise if anybody is allowed the freedom to start improvement projects on their own accord. You shouldn't go to the other extreme of a completely totalitarian regime where no personal initiative is appreciated—you need the organization to be creative and constantly see new opportunities and solutions. What we mean is that for projects beyond a certain size, time- or moneywise, there should be some kind of improvement board sanctioning the most worthwhile projects. Thus, the type of waiting list we have mentioned can be the logical input for this board. Encourage improvement actions within a business process that do not require any additional personnel (beyond what is already present inside the process), do not require any larger investments, or cannot jeopardize the daily running of the process.

Improvement board

An improvement project is started by either having an improvement board prioritize among processes on a waiting list or initiate one from within a separate process At this initial stage, performance data from the measurement system are usually very useful. To figure out what is causing the less-than-desired performance of the process, a root cause analysis into its symptoms, problems, and reasons for occurrence is the best starting point. For this analysis, the performance data are invaluable in disclosing cause-and-effect relationships and allowing you to probe deeper than the surface symptoms you observe. An electric installation company we worked with experienced problems with infrequent cycles of over- and undercapacity on the part of the service technicians, as indicated by the delivery performance data from their rather crude performance measurement system. At first, they believed the problem was connected to technician absenteeism, poor planning of jobs that could have been handled by one team instead of two or three, and or perhaps not enough service vans. By correlating delivery performance data with weather data, it turned out that capacity dipped dramatically during thunder and lightning storms, and the problem was solved by increasing capacity in periods of severe weather.

Root cause analysis

Once the root cause analysis has provided you with insight into the problems and their possible solutions, specific improvement actions should be planned and implemented, as was accomplished in the example above. When these are in place—or even during their implementation, if that takes some time—the measurement system again comes in handy to make post-implementation measurements. These are used to determine whether improvement actions produced the expected results, whether the performance levels are now acceptable, or if more improvement is required. Sometimes this can be done using existing performance indicators; in other cases, new indicators must be defined to capture the improvement effects.

In our example, changing the work schedules of the service technicians required some negotiations with the union and was not fully in place until nine months after the problem was discovered. During this period, the performance data showed a gradual trend in the right direction, but not as steep as expected. Three months after implementation, however, the performance exceeded expectations. If this happens in your case, then the improvement project is closed; if not, a new round of further analysis and subsequent improvements might be warranted.

There are numerous good books on the market dealing with both root cause analysis and the broader subject of business process improvement, and some of these are listed in the literature section (chapter 14).

13.6 PERFORMANCE DATA ANALYSIS TOOLS

Easy-to-apply data analysis tools

Under this very last heading of the main body of the book, we have included a very small selection of some data analysis tools that you might find useful when subjecting the performance data from your new system to some closer examination—beyond merely looking at the indicators. There are an incredible number of different analysis tools and techniques that can be used in the most unique situations. Some of these are highly complex and require an in-depth understanding of mathematics and statistics, others are merely based on designing a simple, graphical image of your data and judging them subjectively. Since this is not a book about various intriguing analysis methods, we have limited the selection to a small handful of tools that, in our experience, are fairly easy to apply and produce new insight and results:

- Trend analysis, a very simple chart that produces a visual image of the trend, if any is present, of a data set

- Spider chart, another chart type that allows comparison of performance levels for different performance measurements and from different sources

- Performance matrix, used to determine which performance indicators or other aspects of the "performance picture" of a process are important to maximize and improve

- Pareto chart, another visual tool that can be used to illustrate which dominant causes are behind the performance levels you observe

- Scatter chart, which can be used to identify relationships between factors of the performance data

Please note that these tools are probably a notch above the most basic chart types and analysis tools. In many cases, a very crude bar or pie chart can perhaps help you to glean some meaning from your data. We take it for granted, however, that there is no need for presenting such simple approaches here. What the tools we present have in common is that they are based on performance data from the measurement system; thus, we will not address this aspect in the individual treatments below.

Trend Analysis

Trend analysis is, as the name implies, simply developmental analysis over time of the performance level of the indicators in question. By comparing the last measurement with previous ones, it is possible to form an opinion of the direction of the development and sometimes even extrapolate to predict future levels. The latter is rarely very accurate, however, and the main application is to spot trends to enable staying on top of any type of development, be it positive or negative. This is part of the early warning function of your performance measurement system that we talked about earlier (see Figure 2.2), as an indication of a negative trend usually appears before the performance level reaches an unacceptably low level, thus allowing you to counteract the development at an early stage.

There is really nothing very fancy or complex about trend analysis—the main point is to include a sufficient amount of historical data to create a credible trend image. If not enough earlier measurements are included and minor fluctuations are interpreted as a trend, then you make the unfortunate mistake of tampering with a process that is only displaying normal variation. Provided there is enough historical data available, the performance indicator readings are plotted in a simple diagram like the example shown in Figure 13.6. Time is assigned to the horizontal axis, which places the most recent measurement at the far end; the performance level is tracked on the vertical axis; and the available data is plotted to form trend lines.

Sufficient amounts of historical data are required to allow meaningful trend analysis

In Figure 13.6, three performance indicators are included. Of course, it is possible to use separate diagrams for each indicator or include all indicators for one business process in one diagram. The advantage of including

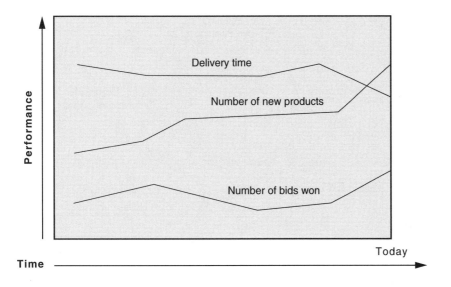

Figure 13.6 Trend analysis diagram.

several indicators in the same chart is that it allows identification of any covariance between the indicators, that is, that they either develop in rhythm with or in anti-phase of each other. This can also be important information, as there might be a cause-and-effect relationship between them.

Spider Chart

Ways to use a spider chart

While trend analysis renders it possible to compare the current performance level to previous measurements, the spider chart is an analysis tool offering additional capabilities for graphically displaying your performance data. It is more of a general chart type that has many applications, but in this respect, there are primarily two useful ways to employ a spider chart:

1. To gain a quick overview of the performance levels for a number of different performance indicators simultaneously, mainly to find which are in order and which are lagging.

2. To compare the organization's own performance level to that of other organizations—a graphical presentation of benchmarking data.

Figure 13.7 shows an example of a spider chart for the business process of product development. Each spoke in the chart represents one performance indicator for this process. Obviously, it is also possible to let the

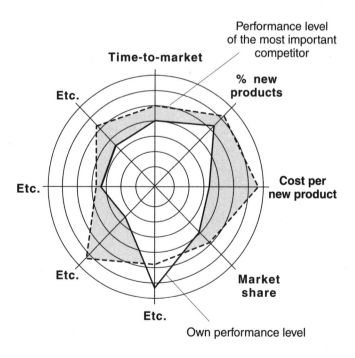

Figure 13.7 Example of a spider chart.

spokes represent processes and design one chart to represent an overall view of the entire organization. The performance level is indicated by plotting a point on the spoke that shows where the performance level rises as the radius increases. This means that the farther from the center of the chart the point is placed, the better the performance. For each spoke, the relevant unit of measurement for the performance level is used. This will give different units of measurement for the individual spokes, but this does not cause any problems. The main purpose is to create some type of performance profile, which is accomplished by drawing lines between the points in the chart.

Performance profile

By plotting the performance level of both your own organization and the level of one or more other organizations, an image is formed of how well you compare. Depending on where the gap with competitors is the largest, you can select the business processes that should be improved.

Performance Matrix

The main problem with employing the spider chart for deciding which performance indicators or business processes to improve is that all entries included in the chart are assigned equal weight. Based on the spider chart, the mechanical approach is simply to conclude that the process needing improvement has the largest gap between the benchmarking partners. To balance this picture, the performance matrix adds the importance factor to the picture. This supplements the two preceding tools, which focus on performance alone. Using the performance matrix with the other tools can avoid wasting resources to improve processes that are performing poorly and are also not very important.

Adding the dimension of importance

An example of a performance matrix is shown in Figure 13.8. The matrix is divided into four quadrants, with importance placed along the horizontal axis and the current performance level along the vertical. The performance indicators to be analyzed are plotted in the matrix based on performance data from the measurement system and a subjective evaluation of their importance. The meaning of the four quadrants is as follows:

The four quadrants of the performance matrix

- Unimportant (low importance, low performance): Although the performance level is low, the low importance renders it unnecessary to invest any resources into improvement.

- Overkill (low importance, high performance): The performance level is high, but this is of less consequence since the elements in this quadrant are not especially important to the organization's competitiveness. Therefore, this is not a candidate for improvement.

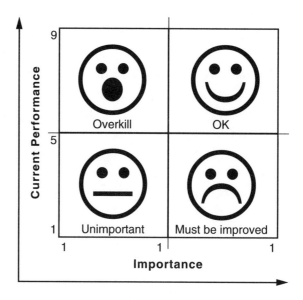

Figure 13.8 Basic performance matrix template.

- Must be improved (high importance, low performance): This is the obvious area for starting improvements. The performance indicators or business processes that fall within this area are important, but the current performance level is low.

- OK (high importance, high performance): A golden rule is that areas where the performance is already good can still be improved. However, the elements that, in addition to being important, are not performing well today (must be improved) should be improved first. If no processes fall within this quadrant, processes in the OK quadrant can be relevant candidates for improvement efforts.

Pareto Chart

The 80–20 rule   The Pareto chart is based on the so-called Pareto principle, formulated by the Italian mathematician Vilfredo Pareto in the 1800s. He was concerned with the distribution of the riches in society, and claimed that 20 percent of the population owned 80 percent of the wealth. Translated into modern quality terminology, the Pareto principle states that most of the effects, often around 80 percent, are caused by a small number of causes, often only 20 percent. For example, usually 80 percent of the problems related to purchased material are caused by 20 percent of the suppliers. Even more importantly, 80 percent of all costs connected to poor quality or generally low performance are caused by 20 percent of all possible causes. A healthy approach is therefore to start the improvement work by attacking these 20 percent, which are often labeled "the vital few." This does not imply that the remaining 80 percent should be ignored; these "important many" should, in due time, also be addressed. The Pareto principle only suggests the order in which problems should be attacked.

The Pareto chart itself is a tool used to display this skewed distribution graphically, the so-called 80–20 rule. The chart shows the causes to a problem sorted by the degree of seriousness and expressed as frequency of occurrence, costs, performance level, and so on. Causes are sorted placing the most severe on the left-hand side of the chart, rendering it quite easy to identify the vital few. To portray further information in the chart, it is common practice to also include a curve showing cumulative importance. This is depicted in Figure 13.9.

A quick inspection of the chart can answer such questions as: What are the two to three main causes for the low performance level of this process? Or, How large a portion of the costs can be attributed to the most vital causes? This information can be used for actively directing improvement efforts toward areas that are likely to produce the best effects.

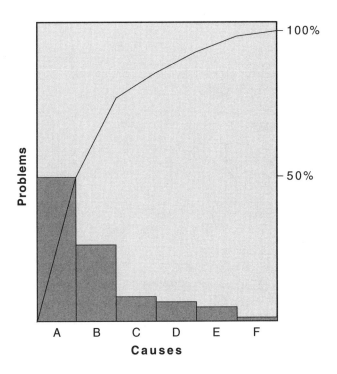

Figure 13.9   A general Pareto chart with a line for cumulative importance.

Scatter Chart

The relationship between two variables

A scatter chart can be used to show the relationship between two variables. Variables can be process characteristics, performance indicators, or other conditions, and are usually measured at specified time intervals. When one factor increases, the other can either increase, decrease, or display only random variation. If the two variables seem to change in synchronization, it might mean that they are related to and impact each other. For example, we could find that the number of defects increases in proportion with the amount of overtime used.

The relationship between the variables being examined can range from a highly positive to a highly negative correlation. Between these two extremes, there are weaker degrees of both positive and negative correlation, as well as no correlation at all. Figure 13.10 shows some examples of different scatter charts for different degrees of correlation.

A scatter chart can confirm or invalidate the suspicion that there might be a connection between different performance indicators, both for the same business process or even for different processes. If two indicators do work together, this is useful information if you plan to improve one of the processes or detect early warnings of a negative trend in one of them.

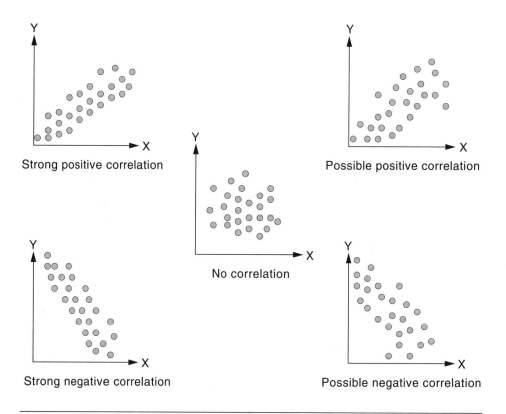

Figure 13.10 Different scatter charts showing different degrees of correlation.

13.7 THE BEST OF LUCK

Well, that is basically all that we have to tell you about designing and implementing your state-of-the-art performance measurement system. We took you through some introductory motivation regarding the benefits and applications of performance measurement, as well as some of the problems with such systems. The main body of the book is the eight-step process for designing a performance measurement system, and we provided you with some ideas on how to use the system once it is implemented.

We would again like to emphasize that this approach is just one of many ways of going about this design process. If our way can give you some inspiration for your future efforts, we have achieved our goal. Our design process has been used in quite a few projects so far, and we constantly make refinements to improve and update it. As we have mentioned before, if you gain further insight into the design of performance measurement systems or have specific experiences with this process, we would be truly grateful if you could bring it to our attention.

We welcome any suggestions for improvements of the performance measurement system design process

All that remains now is to wish you the very best of luck in your endeavors to design and implement your own state-of-the-art performance measurement system—we truly hope you succeed and that it will bring you many positive outcomes!

References and Recommended Literature

If you are accustomed to reading more academic literature than what we have aimed for here, then you have probably noticed the absence of literature references scattered throughout the text. This has been a deliberate choice on our part, as our main objective has been to instill sufficient knowledge in you to develop and implement your own state-of-the-art performance measurement system. However, since we recognize that once you get into this very exciting topic, you will probably want to go further in your studies, we have provided some key references that are worth looking up:

Andersen, Bjørn, and Per-Gaute Pettersen. *The Benchmarking Handbook— Step-by-Step Instructions.* London: Chapman & Hall, 1996.

Andersen, Bjørn. *Business Process Improvement Toolbox.* Milwaukee: ASQ Quality Press, 1998.

Andersen, Bjørn, and Tom Fagerhaug. *Root Cause Analysis: Simplified Tools and Techniques.* Milwaukee: ASQ Quality Press, 1999.

Brandenburger, Adam M., and Barry J. Nalebuff. *Co-opetition.* New York: HarperCollinsBusiness, 1996.

Camp, Robert C. *Benchmarking: The Search for Industry Best Practices That Lead to Superior Performance.* Milwaukee: ASQC Quality Press, 1989.

Camp, Robert C. *Business Process Benchmarking: Finding and Implementing Best Practices.* Milwaukee: ASQC Quality Press, 1994.

Camp, Robert C. *Global Cases in Benchmarking: Best Practices from Organizations around the World.* Milwaukee: ASQ Quality Press, 1998.

Conti, Tito. *Organizational Self-Assessment.* London: Chapman & Hall, 1997.

Deming, W. E. *Out of the Crisis: Quality, Productivity, and Competitive Position.* Cambridge, MA: Cambridge University Press, 1986.

Driscoll, D. M., and W. M. Hoffman. *Ethics Matters: How to Implement Values-Driven Management.* Waltham, MA: Bentley College, Center for Business Excellence, 2000.

Galloway, D. *Mapping Work Processes.* Milwaukee: ASQC Quality Press, 1994.

Hammer, M., and J. Champy. Reengineering the Corporation: A Manifesto for Business Revolution. New York: Harper Business, 1993.,

Harrington, H. J. *Business Process Improvement: The Breakthrough Strategy for Total Quality, Productivity, and Competitiveness.* New York: McGraw-Hill, 1991.

Hronec, Steven M. *Vital Signs: Using Quality, Time, and Cost Performance Measurements to Chart Your Company's Future.* New York: Amacom, 1993.

Johnson, H. T., and R. S. Kaplan. *Relevance Lost: The Rise and Fall of Management Accounting.* Boston: Harvard Business School Press, 1987.

Kaplan, R. S., ed. *Measures for Manufacturing Excellence.* Boston: Harvard Business School Press, 1990.

Kaplan, R. S., and D. P. Norton. *The Balanced Scorecard.* Boston: Harvard Business School Press, 1996.

Kaydos, W. *Operational Performance Measurement: Increasing Total Productivity.* Boca Raton, FL: St. Lucie Press, 1999.

King, A. M. "Green Dollars and Blue Dollars: The Paradox of Cost Reduction." *Journal of Cost Management,* no. 7 (1993): 44–52.

Lynch, R. L., and K. C. Cross. *Measure Up! Yardstick for Continuous Improvement.* Cambridge, MA: Blackwell Business, 1991.

Maskell, B. H. *Performance Measurement for World Class Manufacturing.* Cambridge, MA: Productivity Press, 1991.

Peters, T. J., and R. H. Waterman Jr. *In Search of Excellence: Lessons from America's Best-Run Companies.* New York: Harper & Row, 1982.

Rolstadås, Asbjørn, ed. *Performance Management: A Business Process Benchmarking Approach.* London: Chapman & Hall, 1995.

Sink, D. S., and T. C. Tuttle. *Planning and Measurement in Your Organization of the Future.* Norcross, VA: Industrial Engineering and Management Press, 1989.

Appendix

Suggestions for Performance Indicators

In the main section of this book, we have assembled quite an extensive set of possible performance indicators. This set is not supposed to be a holistic, comprehensive list covering every imaginable aspect, but rather selected suggestions based on experience and different sources. The intention behind these is not that you should copy them uncritically, but that they can serve as inspiration when you are struggling with the details of your own performance indicators in Step 4 of the design process.

There are many different sources for these sample performance indicators, from enterprises we have worked with, to the SCOR model of supply chain management, to research projects and other literature. As you will see, we have tried to group them by business process and organizational area, following the same headings as in chapter 8 and Figure 8.2. Since these indicators are so different in type and nature, however, we have not made any attempts at structuring them in any other way. We should also point out that in the original sources, there are often more detailed descriptions of the indicators, as well as formulas for calculating them. Both to avoid stifling your creativity and having you directly copy detailed indicators tailored to other organizations, we have chosen to omit these here. We believe the mostly self-explanatory "titles" of the indicators are sufficient to illustrate what types of indicators can be used for various business processes and areas.

If you have suggestions for other indicators that you use successfully in your own organization or that you think are missing in this overview, do not hesitate to let us know!

PROCUREMENT AND INBOUND LOGISTICS

- Incoming material quality
- Number of supply sources
- Supplier volume flexibility
- Percent of parts delivered to point of use
- Supplier fill rate
- Supplier on-time delivery
- Supplier payment timeliness
- Material acquisition costs

MANUFACTURING/ SERVICE PROVISION

- Manufacturing volume flexibility
- Manufacturing mix flexibility
- Actual-to-theoretical cycle time
- Order fulfillment costs
- Percent of parts delivered to point of use
- Complete time from manufacture to order ready to ship
- Work-in-progress as percentage of turnover
- Inventory obsolescence as percentage of total inventory
- Batch changeover time
- Capacity utilization

OUTBOUND LOGISTICS/INSTALLATION

- Number of orders delivered as incomplete
- Number of orders with complete and accurate documentation
- Percentage of faultless installations
- Delivery performance to agreed delivery date
- Distribution costs
- Finished goods inventory
- Installation costs
- Transportation costs

AFTER-SALES SERVICE

- Percentage of warranty cases and returns
- Average lead time for repairs
- Cost of after-sales service ratio to turnover
- Warranty costs
- Number of requests handled or solved at first contact
- Product return cost ratio
- Average complaints handling resolution time

SALES

- Number of callbacks as percentage of total inquiries

- Tendering bid ratio

- Lost accounts (retention rate)

- Days of sales outstanding

- Number of customer requests that result in sales

- Percentage of EDI transactions (electronic data interchange)

- Customer order acquisition costs

- Order entry and maintenance costs

- Order entry complete to order ready for shipment time

MARKETING

- Market share for main product

- Contribution of new products

- Advertising/promotion cost ratio to turnover

- Customer base growth

- Ratio of potential customers or users who know the organization's products or services

- Media references to, or articles about, the organization

- Customer dependency

- Number of seminars, information campaigns, direct marketing, and so on, performed

- Ratio of new customer return

- Ratio of customer visits

INVOICING AND PAYMENT

- Faultless invoices

- Outstanding invoices older than 60 days

- Customer invoicing/accounting costs

- Customer payment timeliness

- Percentage of credit notes of invoices issued

FINANCIAL MANAGEMENT

- Return on assets

- Cash-to-cash cycle time

- Asset turns

- Overhead cost

- Purchased materials ratio

- Personnel wages ratio

- Return on equity

- Value added per full-time equivalent employee

- Solvency ratio

- Gross margin ratio

- Depreciation ratio

- Budget accuracy

- Work-in-progress inventory ratio

- Capital turnover ratio

- Finished goods inventory ratio

HUMAN RESOURCE MANAGEMENT AND DEVELOPMENT

- Indirect to direct labor headcount ratio

- Employee turnover

- Percentage of performance reviews conducted by deadline

- Training hours per employee

- Employees who have completed a personal development plan

- Employees certified for skilled functions or positions

- Employees' ability to perform several jobs/functions

- Employees terminated for performance or other problems

- Recruitment lead time

MANAGEMENT OF SAFETY, HEALTH, AND ENVIRONMENT

- Ratio of person-days lost due to injuries

- Ratio of person-days lost due to sickness

- Number of emergency drills

- Percentage of employees trained in the crisis handling plan

- Percentage of employees trained in safety procedures

- Employee absenteeism

MAINTENANCE

- Machine availability

- Machine reliability

- Total system downtime

- Preventive to reactive maintenance ratio

- Service level for spare parts inventory

- Total maintenance cost

- Percentage of employees with basic maintenance skills

- Percentage of resources with dedicated resource owners

RESOURCE MANAGEMENT

- Investment level in production machinery and equipment

- Average length of service for employees

- Average age of buildings

- Total resource management costs ratio to turnover

- Average age of employees

- Average age of computers and computer programs

- Information system operating costs

- Percentage increase/decrease in the value of the organization's overall resources

- Average age of core production machinery and equipment

- Investment level in buildings

PROJECT MANAGEMENT

- Percentage budget deviation
- Percentage schedule deviation
- Percentage of employees with basic project management skills
- Project goal achievement ratio
- Percentage of completed projects assessed for experience transfer
- Average number of projects per employee

QUALITY MANAGEMENT

- Percentage defective parts/services with faults
- Poor quality costs
- Scrap expense
- Percentage rework
- Percentage of employees with quality management training

CONTINUOUS IMPROVEMENT

- Improvement suggestions per employee
- Improvement cost ratio to turnover
- Number of improvements accomplished
- Incentive ratio to average salary
- Savings to improvement cost ratio
- Percentage of employees in self-managing teams

NEW PRODUCT/SERVICE DEVELOPMENT

- Average product/service development lead time
- Patents filed, issued, or incorporated into products
- New product/service turnover
- New product/service development cost
- Proportion of people involved in product/service development
- Number of new products/services
- Number of refined products/services
- Percentage new product/service development projects completed on time
- Percentage new product/service development projects completed on budget
- Product/service development costs ratio to turnover

SUPPLIER BASE DEVELOPMENT

- Number of active suppliers
- Average supplier turnover
- Supplier assessment ratio
- Percentage of new product/service development projects conducted in cooperation with suppliers
- Percentage single source parts
- Supplier development cost ratio to turnover

PRODUCTION/SERVICE TECHNOLOGY DEVELOPMENT

- Average process development lead time

- Production/service technology development costs ratio to turnover

- Ratio of employees involved in production/service technology development

- Number of new production or service processes

- Number of refined production or service processes

STRATEGIC PLANNING

- Strategic plan refinement frequency

- Ratio of employees involved in the strategic planning process

- Average strategic planning duration

- Strategic planning cost ratio to turnover

- Strategic plan achievement

EXTERNAL ENVIRONMENT

- Recyclable components

- Green product sales ratio

- Percentage of enabling innovations for environmentally superior products/services

- Percentage of environmentally aware suppliers

- Percentage of packaging recycled per unit of product

- External emissions during operation

- Percentage of suppliers with an implemented or a certified environmental management system

- Energy cost

- Average quantity of waste produced per unit of product

ETHICS

- Management wages to industry average ratio

- Worker wages to industry average ratio

- Percentage of suppliers with fair trade policies

- Cost recovery pricing level

- Number of customer complaints based on ethical issues

- Percentage of employees aware of the organization's ethical policies

STAKEHOLDER INTERFACES

Under this heading, we include principally any stakeholder, but the more critical ones to measure are probably suppliers, shareholders/owners, customers, employees, and society in general.

- Dependability of most important suppliers

- The suppliers' ability to contribute to the organization's competitiveness

- Fulfillment of shareholder expectations for return on investments

- Ratio of resources applied to support community environmental programs to turnover

- Availability of labor in the community

- Availability of infrastructure in the community

- Customer satisfaction index

- Customer turnover

- Dependability of most important customers

- Number of recognition events and awards bestowed upon employees

- Number of employees who will retire during the next five years

- Employee turnover

SUPPLY CHAIN

For supply chain measurement, many of the same performance indicators used at the individual enterprise level will apply, in an aggregated version.

- Total supply chain logistics costs

- Total supply chain delivery performance to end customer

- Total supply chain quality complaints from end customer

- Total supply chain volume flexibility

- Total supply chain mix flexibility

- Product/component recycling level of the supply chain

Index